MW01167385

Spies

Other Books in the History Makers Series:

History MAKERS

Spies

By Diane Yancey

Lucent Books
P.O. Box 289011, San Diego, CA 92198-9011

Library of Congress Cataloging-in-Publication Data

Yancey, Diane.
  Spies / by Diane Yancey.
     p.   cm. — (History makers)
  Includes bibliographical references and index.
  Summary: Discusses the history of spying, famous spies, and the
  technological future of spying.
  ISBN 1-56006-958-9 (hardcover)
  1. Espionage—Juvenile literature. 2. Spies—Biography—Juvenile
  literature. [1. Espionage. 2. Spies.] I. Title. II. Series.
  UB270.5 .Y35 2002
  327.12—dc21

2001003196

CONTENTS

FOREWORD

The literary form most often referred to as "multiple biography" was perfected in the first century A.D. by Plutarch, a perceptive and talented moralist and historian who hailed from the small town of Chaeronea in central Greece. His most famous work, *Parallel Lives*, consists of a long series of biographies of noteworthy ancient Greek and Roman statesmen and military leaders. Frequently, Plutarch compares a famous Greek to a famous Roman, pointing out similarities in personality and achievements. These expertly constructed and very readable tracts provided later historians and others, including playwrights like Shakespeare, with priceless information about prominent ancient personages and also inspired new generations of writers to tackle the multiple biography genre.

The Lucent History Makers series proudly carries on the venerable tradition handed down from Plutarch. Each volume in the series consists of a set of five to eight biographies of important and influential historical figures who were linked together by a common factor. In *Rulers of Ancient Rome*, for example, all the figures were generals, consuls, or emperors of either the Roman Republic or Empire; while the subjects of *Fighters Against American Slavery*, though they lived in different places and times, all shared the same goal, namely the eradication of human servitude. Mindful that politicians and military leaders are not (and never have been) the only people who shape the course of history, the editors of the series have also included representatives from a wide range of endeavors, including scientists, artists, writers, philosophers, religious leaders, and sports figures.

Each book is intended to give a range of figures—some well known, others less known; some who made a great impact on history, others who made only a small impact. For instance, by making Columbus's initial voyage possible, Spain's Queen Isabella I, featured in *Women Leaders of Nations*, helped to open up the New World to exploration and exploitation by the European powers. Unarguably, therefore, she made a major contribution to a series of events that had momentous consequences for the entire world. By contrast, Catherine II, the eighteenth-century Russian queen, and Golda Meir, the modern Israeli prime minister, did not play roles of global impact; however, their policies and actions significantly influenced the historical development of both their own countries and their regional neighbors. Regardless of their relative importance in the greater historical scheme, all of the figures chronicled in the History Makers series made contributions to posterity; and their public achievements, as well as what is known about their private lives, are presented and evaluated in light of the most recent scholarship.

In addition, each volume in the series is documented and substantiated by a wide array of primary and secondary source quotations. The primary source quotes enliven the text by presenting eyewitness views of the times and culture in which each history maker lived; while the secondary source quotes, taken from the works of respected modern scholars, offer expert elaboration and/ or critical commentary. Each quote is footnoted, demonstrating to the reader exactly where biographers find their information. The footnotes also provide the reader with the means of conducting additional research. Finally, to further guide and illuminate readers, each volume in the series features photographs, two bibliographies, and a comprehensive index.

The History Makers series provides both students engaged in research and more casual readers with informative, enlightening, and entertaining overviews of individuals from a variety of circumstances, professions, and backgrounds. No doubt all of them, whether loved or hated, benevolent or cruel, constructive or destructive, will remain endlessly fascinating to each new generation seeking to identify the forces that shaped their world.

The Second Oldest Profession

Hear the word "spy," and a variety of images come to mind. One is the sexy, daredevil James Bond character who gets in and out of dangerous situations by using an assortment of high-tech gadgets. Another is the glamorous Mata Hari spy who vamps men while sneaking top secret documents from their inside breast pockets. A third is the blank-faced, trench-coated agent who stands under a lamppost and whispers secrets to a fellow conspirator on a foggy night.

In real life, spies—people who steal secret information from an enemy or competitor—are somewhat different from these stereotypes. They usually look like scientists, businesspeople, military officers, or diplomats, and try to appear as ordinary as everyone else while carrying out their covert activities. After all, their survival and success depend on remaining unnoticed. "Their lives are to some extent ghost-like. Even if they themselves can be seen, their real purpose must remain unseen," writes one intelligence expert.[1] Those spies who are conspicuous—like Mata Hari or the glamorous Belle Boyd of the Civil War, for instance—come to grief. Boyd was imprisoned; Mata Hari ended up in front of a firing squad.

Who Spies?

All kinds of people spy. Spies have been male, female, old, young, free, slave, wealthy, and poor. The best are usually likable, able to get what they want by charm or the force of their personality. But if a spy has other necessary qualifications—steady nerves, natural cunning, a good intellect, and plenty of courage—he (or she) can be eccentric, inconsiderate, or downright unlikable, and still succeed. "The qualities that go to make a great spy are almost indefinable," states author Donald McCormick. "In any case they vary from one individual to another."[2]

Many historical figures have been spies. Spying is said to be the second oldest profession in the world, prostitution being the first. Spies can also be as up-to-date as today's news. One of the most recent cases is that of alleged spy Robert Hanssen, who was arrested by the FBI in February 2001 for selling secrets to Russia. Hanssen was a professional agent, but most spies have been amateurs—people who were in the right place at the right time to steal information. Only in the twentieth century did espionage organizations set up "spy schools" where spies could get formal training in tradecraft—techniques such as meeting a contact, eluding a tail, and so forth. Some of the largest and best-known organizations to have spy schools were the United States' Central Intelligence Agency (CIA), Britain's Secret Intelligence Service (SIS), East Germany's Ministerium für Staatssicherheit (Stasi), and the Soviet Union's Komitet Gosudarstvennoy Bezopasnosti (KGB).

Not even the best schools can teach everything an agent needs to know to successfully steal industrial, military, or technological secrets, however. A combination of technique plus luck, audacity, and ingenuity is needed if he or she is to get the goods and not be caught.

People often think of spies, such as Mata Hari (left) and James Bond, as being provocative and glamorous.

Experience can also turn a good spy into a great one. "Espionage is very often a matter of intuition plus experience," McCormick points out.[3]

Why Spy?

Whether amateur or professional, people spy for a variety of reasons. Many are highly patriotic. Some are strongly committed to a political philosophy. A few work for the thrill they get from taking risks. Many more spy out of greed. Billions of dollars a year have been spent (and are still being spent) to support spies who are willing to steal the secrets of a government, company, or research department for cash or regular deposits into a bank account in Switzerland.

Some spies work to protect their country and their agency from enemy espionage. This activity is termed counterespionage. Counterespionage agents often try to prevent the theft of secret information rather than go out to steal it from others. They try to detect the presence of enemy spies in their midst. Counterespionage is the most complex aspect of spying, since the utmost cunning, deviousness, and duplicity are necessary to outwit and outmaneuver other spies. The hardest spies to catch are counterespionage agents, be-

Julius and Ethel Rosenberg never spoke publicly about their years as spies for the Soviets.

cause they are well versed in all the crosses and double crosses that spies use to avoid detection.

The information that spies steal is termed intelligence. It can help win wars, impact national security, or uncover the strengths and weaknesses of an opposing espionage agency. The intelligence that CIA spy Aldrich Ames supplied to the Soviets during the 1980s, for example, did immeasurable harm to U.S. intelligence services. Sometimes the value of intelligence can be questionable, however. Such was the case of Julius and Ethel Rosenberg, whose stolen information about the atomic bomb did not significantly help the Soviets.

Cloak of Mystery

Because spies are devious and prone to lying, writing their biographies is difficult. One author says, "The secret world of intelligence is surrounded by mystique. The very nature of espionage makes it a difficult subject to research and it is often well-nigh [nearly] impossible to establish exactly what took place during a particular event."[4]

Such is the case with the biographies included here. Sidney Reilly, for instance, wove such a cloak of mystery around his life that even his spymasters were not sure that they knew his true identity, his history, or his loyalties. The Rosenbergs went to their deaths with their lips sealed, so the details of much of their story remain untold. Even when secret agents write their own biographies, they shade, embellish, omit, and rearrange events. Sometimes they do this to make a case more exciting. Sometimes they lie to put their actions in a better light. Sometimes they are guarding information that still remains secret.

Despite the difficulties, the lives of eight spies are recounted in the following pages. They are unique in more ways than one. Donald McCormick observes, "We [may be] very close to witnessing the end of the era of the great individual spy. Team work, the assessing of reports from several agents and even the advent of the computer have all tended to create less scope for the single agent."[5] If such is the case, these eight represent a vanishing breed of men and women who were cagey, independent, and intrepid. All knew the risks they were taking. All paid a price for their clandestine activities. Such was their fate. Such is the fate of most spies.

CHAPTER 1

Mrs. Barnes

A successful spy is someone who can gather vast amounts of useful information without being discovered or captured. By such standards, Ann Bates was a very successful spy. In fact, author John Bakeless, an expert on military intelligence during the Revolutionary War, says that Ann Bates "may justly be described as the most successful female spy in history."[6] Bates performed many daring exploits during the Revolution. But she hid her accomplishments under a mantle of obscurity and has remained unnoticed and overlooked for more than two hundred years.

Humble Beginnings

Born in Pennsylvania about 1748, Ann was an intelligent child who grew up to become a schoolteacher. At some point she married Joseph Bates (or Beats), an armorer (a weapons maintenance and repairman) in the British army. Neither husband nor wife earned much in their chosen occupation, so Ann supplemented their income by running a small store, keeping bees, and raising sheep.

When war broke out between Great Britain and the American colonies in 1775, the Bateses were two of many Americans who remained loyal to England and King George III. There were thousands of these so-called Loyalists or Tories in America during this period, and they came from all social classes and occupations. Their numbers were greatest in the colonies of New York, Pennsylvania, Georgia, and the Carolinas.

The British occupied the Bateses' hometown of Philadelphia, Pennsylvania, in 1777, but Continental (or American) forces captured the city in 1778. About that time, Ann Bates decided to leave. Her husband was on the battlefield with the British army, she was alone, and she had to hide her Loyalist leanings unless she wanted to be persecuted by her neighbors. More important, however, she had been approached by John Cregge (or Craigie), a civilian involved in British intelligence. How she met him is unrecorded, but he must have recognized that her brains and courage were being wasted on raising bees and sheep. He asked her to visit him if she came to New York. Perhaps there would be some work she could do there for the Loyalist cause.

Spying for King George

Cregge must have hinted that he had work of a covert nature for Bates to carry out. If not, her next action was extremely farsighted. Before leaving Philadelphia, she paid a visit to the commander of the Continental forces in Philadelphia, Benedict Arnold. (Arnold had not yet become a traitor to the American cause.) Pretending to be sympathetic to his side, she asked him for a pass to General George Washington's camp near White Plains, New York. It was an item that she had no intention of using immediately, but that would prove valuable later on. Arnold obliged, and Bates then set out for New York City. No record shows whether she traveled by wagon, on horseback, or on foot.

Bates reached New York, then held by the British, about the end of June 1778. She was directed to a Major Duncan Drummond, aide to Sir Henry Clinton. Clinton was commander of all British forces in North America in 1778, and was desperate for

Even during the Revolutionary War there were spies including Ann Bates, a British Loyalist.

information about Washington and the Continental army's movements.

With her pass and her willingness to serve as a spy, Bates seemed to be a godsend to Drummond. Unwilling to make her task too difficult, he directed her to travel to Washington's camp and contact a Tory spy there. The spy was a disloyal American officer who would brief her on American troop strength and positions. Bates was to bring the information back to Drummond. In order to identify herself to the spy, she was given a secret token. This token remained so secret that no one ever learned

General George Washington, who had information Ann Bates wanted.

what it was. Drummond also assigned her the code name "Mrs. Barnes."

The Peddler

Carefully considering her situation, Bates decided to pose as a peddler, someone who traveled from place to place selling small articles. Peddlers were such familiar figures at the time that they could come and go at will without being noticed. Clinton himself approved her scheme, and she was given five guineas (gold coins) for expenses. Purchasing a variety of articles such as medicinal rhubarb, thread, needles, combs, and knives, she bundled up her pack and set out.

Like most peddlers, Bates traveled on foot, hitching rides on passing wagons when she could. The road to White Plains was rough and long, especially because she went by a roundabout route so no one would suspect she had come from British headquarters in New York. Once, finding that a bridge was out near the town of Trenton, New Jersey, she risked her life fording a river whose water came up to her armpits. After four days of travel, she arrived at her destination on July 2, 1778.

Bad news awaited her in the Continental camp, however. The spy she was to meet had resigned from the army. She was left with no contact, and no source of information. Undaunted, Bates decided to gather the information herself.

Dividing her wares into portions so they would not be purchased too quickly, she moved through the camps, selling, observing, and noting what she saw. Because of her husband's job, she was familiar with war weaponry and thus could report on it with some expertise. She later said, "I had the Opportunity of going through their whole Army Remarking at the same time the strength & Situation of each Brigade, & the Number of Cannon with their Situation and Weight of Ball each Cannon was Charged

Ann Bates disguised herself as a peddler like the one shown here to remain unidentified during her travels.

with."[7] Bates also left the camp with information regarding Continental troop movements and the existence of special troops detailed to intercept British patrols.

Setbacks

Bates's journey back to New York proved that the danger of exposure was ever-present. Because the country was at war, and because many spies posed as peddlers during that time, she was arrested and detained as a suspicious person. Under the watchful eyes of a female patriot, she had to remove her clothes and submit to a search. To Bates's chagrin, the woman confiscated a pair of silver shoe buckles, a silver thimble, and some money. Somehow, Bates managed to conceal her secret token.

After being held by the enemy for a day and a night, Bates was set free. As soon as possible, she returned to New York and reported to Major Drummond. Impressed with her effectiveness, Drummond allowed her only one day's rest before he asked her to make another foray into Washington's camps. Replenishing her supplies with a second five-guinea allowance, she set off, arriving in the camps about July 29. She had been told to rendezvous with a man named Chambers, but she soon discovered that he had been killed in battle. Again she was left to scout out information on her own.

Selling odds and ends, and wandering throughout the camps for three or four days, Bates gathered a wide variety of information that ranged from the number of cannons set up on a hill to the state of men's uniforms and the quality and quantity of rations they were given. "Shad Fish delivered out twice a Week and other days fresh Provisions—Plenty of Bread and flour . . ." she later reported.[8]

"Timly Information"

Always on the alert, always aware of danger, Bates was under a great deal of stress during her journeys into enemy territory. Certainly she was exhausted on her return. Undoubtedly she was well aware that, if caught, she could face the ultimate punishment of death. She worked uncomplainingly, however, making at least three trips to Washington's camps in the summer of 1778. On her third visit, she found that security had tightened and reported, "it is with the greatest difficulty—any person can get within their camp."[9]

Nevertheless, Bates managed it. By this time Drummond must have been confident that she could gather information on her own, and she proved him correct. In a bold move, she actually went inside

Bates sneaked in to General Washington's camp and obtained information about the army's supplies, rations, and strategies.

Washington's headquarters, where she was able to eavesdrop on an aide and an officer who were exchanging information there. Bates learned that six hundred boats were being prepared for an American landing on Long Island, New York. They would be ready in two weeks. She was memorizing this important information when the officer realized that he was being overheard and changed the subject. "When he look'd Round & saw me a Stranger he turn'd [changed] the Discourse for me to hear," she recalled.[10]

Although she had been noticed in Washington's headquarters, Bates refused to run away before finishing her mission. She spent several more days taking stock of the enemy's weapons—she counted fifty-one guns and five mortars (muzzle-loading cannons), then noted that nine more guns arrived a day later. She noticed that food and other provisions for the troops were scarcer this time. Her most vital piece of news, however, turned out to be the fact that the French Marquis de Lafayette, a major general in the Continental army, had marched to Rhode Island with about five thousand soldiers to await the arrival of the French fleet. The event meant that the French had entered the war on the American side.

Clinton himself was planning an expedition to relieve British forces in Rhode Island, and with Bates's information he was able to strengthen his forces and fortifications and hold out against Continental attacks for another year. Bates later recalled, "My timly information was the blessed means of saving rowd island

[Rhode Island] Garison with all the troops and stores who must otherwise (have) fallen a pray to their Enemies." Major Drummond agreed. "She asserts nothing but what is strictly true," he attested.[11]

Discovered

Bates was given a few weeks to rest after her August mission. In mid-September 1778, however, Washington and his army went on the move, and Drummond once again requested that she find out the Continentals' plans. In her disguise as a peddler, she was still able to get into the enemy ranks. She wisely decided that she would stay close to the column of soldiers led by Washington himself, this "being the likeliest to gain the best Intelligence."[12] Bates stayed with the Army until it neared the Connecticut border; then she turned back and headed for New Jersey and a rendezvous with her contact, John Cregge. After giving him her information, she was directed back to Washington's army to continue to learn the latest news.

Bates had just arrived in the Continental camp again when the unexpected happened. She was recognized by someone who knew her true identity and loyalty—"one Smith a deserter from the 27th (British) Regt," she later wrote. Apparently Smith did not immediately expose her, perhaps because his past loyalties were questionable as well. Bates did not know that, however, and she fled "for fear of being taken up as a Spie."[13] She paused long enough to count the artillery of a nearby brigade of New York Continentals, then headed straight for the safety of the British lines.

New Directions

When Bates reached New York at the end of September, she regretfully told Major Drummond that she "durst not any more attemp't to prosecute discoveries in General Washingtons Army," and Drummond replied that "he did not know what they should do" without her invaluable services. The spy gratefully took his words as "a plain demonstration that I had been Serviceable to the English Army."[14] Although Drummond tried to use Bates in some safer capacity in the region shortly thereafter, his plans fell through and she remained inoperative for a time after that.

Bates could no longer spy in Washington's camps, but she was still useful to the British cause. In late 1778 she stole back into the Philadelphia region where she met a "Friend that was in Connection with General [Benedict] Arnold."[15] By this time Arnold had become disgruntled with his treatment by the Americans in

Even though she had been discovered, Bates took the time to count the New York Continental army's artillery.

the war and was considering changing sides. Bates apparently acted as a liaison in the early negotiations that led to Arnold's linkup with British spymaster John André. Arnold soon transferred his loyalties to the British and plotted to betray his country. The plot fell through when André was captured by the Continentals. André was hanged as a spy in 1780 and Arnold fled to England after the war.

Humble End

In 1780, General Clinton moved south with his forces, and Ann Bates went along, accompanying her husband who was part of the general's artillery force. In South Carolina she probably again served as a spy, but her exploits are unrecorded. In March 1781, Bates and her husband received permission to leave America for England, where they remained for the rest of their lives. The move is unexplained. Perhaps they realized that the British were losing the war and that America would be an uncomfortable place for those who had sided with its enemies.

Little more is known about the life of Ann Bates. Her husband deserted her after a time and she was left alone in England, ill and without money. In desperation she petitioned the British government to pay her a ten-pound pension that had been promised when she served during the war. When they did not reply she wrote bitterly,

Haid I Doon half as much for the Scruff of Mankind I mean the Rabls [Rebels] I should not be thus Left to Parish [perish].—Was I in Amarica Now to share the same fate of my Noble Unfortunate frind Major Andrew (André)—it would be much better for me than to Drawg [drag] out a life Which all Laws humain and Divine forbids me to Putt a Period too.[16]

Finally, Major Drummond came to her assistance. "Her information as to Matter and fact, was far superior to every other intelligence,"[17] he stated when recommending that she receive the pension. The testimony was high praise coming from such a prominent military man. It is unclear, however, whether Bates ever received any money.

Ann Bates died in 1801. Few people know or remember her, but her skill, daring, and accomplishments place her in the ranks of some of the most noteworthy and effective spies in history.

CHAPTER 2

Crazy Bet

War creates the need for spies. When two enemies square off against one another, each wants maximum knowledge of the other's secrets, intentions, strengths, and weaknesses in order to win. In the Civil War, many famous and successful secret agents were women. One of the most unique and colorful to spy for the North was Elizabeth Van Lew, born on October 15, 1818, in Richmond, Virginia.

Southern Belle

The Van Lews were a prominent family in Richmond. They lived in a magnificent three-story mansion that commanded a sweeping view of the city and the nearby James River. They owned land in and out of town. Elizabeth's father, John, was a wealthy hardware merchant. Her mother, Eliza, came from a family that traced its ancestry back to the Revolutionary War. The couple had a large personal library, to which John Van Lew added volumes every year. "My parents were both intellectual & devoted to books," Elizabeth recalled.[18]

Elizabeth Van Lew, who lived in this house in Virginia, was a spy for the North during the Civil War.

When Elizabeth was old enough, her parents sent her to Philadelphia to be educated at a school her mother had attended. Philadelphia was home to many abolitionists, and the young girl heard terrible stories about the abuses that slaves suffered. A serious-minded person, she took these stories to heart and grew to hate the institution of slavery, even though her father owned slaves. Her beliefs eventually set her at odds with most Richmonders. "From the time I knew right from wrong, it was my sad privilege to differ in many things from the perceived opinions and principles in my locality (Richmond). This has made my life intensely sad and earnest," she wrote in her diary just before the war.[19]

Van Lew returned from Philadelphia a polished, well-educated young woman who seemed to be the typical Southern belle— pretty, charming, soft-voiced, and absorbed in home and family. Her blue eyes and dark blond hair won her many male admirers. Appearances were deceptive, however; she was intelligent, strong-willed, outspoken, and interested in politics and national issues. Perhaps due to her outspokenness or perhaps her independent spirit, she never married.

As time passed, Van Lew translated her views on slavery into action. After her father's death, she convinced her mother to free all of the family's slaves. Children or relatives of the Van Lew slaves, owned by others and about to be sold, were also purchased and liberated.

Van Lew differed from typical Southern women in other matters as well. In 1860, civil war loomed on the horizon. While Northerners supported a strong federal government and a unified nation in which slavery had no part, most Southerners were willing to secede from the Union rather than give up their slaves and their states' rights. Elizabeth Van Lew was proud to be a Southerner, but the thought of going to war in support of slavery and secession seemed outrageous. "Think of a community rushing gladly, unrestrainedly, eagerly, into a bloody civil war," she wrote as Virginia voted to secede in April 1861. "Surely madness was upon the people!"[20]

War!

War was declared on April 12, 1861, and Van Lew decided almost immediately that she would do everything in her power to help the Union. She also determined that she was going to do what she could to ease the suffering of Northern soldiers captured during battle. Many of these were held in Richmond's makeshift prisons, among them Libby, Belle Isle, and Castle Thunder. All were overcrowded, primitive facilities where illness and death were everyday occurrences.

Most Southerers, who did not want to give up their states' rights and slaves, preferred to break away from the Union.

Through a combination of persistence and flattery, Van Lew obtained official permission to visit the prisons, carrying food, clothes, bedding, and medicines to Northerners there. Her efforts were highly criticized by Richmonders. They had known of Van Lew's unpopular views on slavery, but they had never dreamed that she would be so disloyal as to aid the enemy. She faced insults and intimidation. "The threats, the scowls, the frowns of an infuriated community—who can write of them? I have had brave men shake their fingers in my face and say terrible things," she said. "We have had threats of being driven away, threats of fire, and threats of death."[21]

Union Spy

There is no record of when Elizabeth Van Lew decided to become a spy for the North. Even before the war began, she wrote letters to Northern friends and officials, keeping them informed of

Southern attitudes and events relating to secession and war. As she talked with Union men in the Richmond prisons, she picked up much information—things they had seen on the battlefield and on the way to prison—that she knew would be useful to the North. With very little effort, she devised ways to smuggle the information out of Richmond and into the hands of Union generals.

In early 1863 she began sending her findings, and her own observations as well, to General George Henry Sharpe, head of the newly created Bureau of Military Intelligence. For a time, Sharpe discounted Van Lew's reports, convinced that no woman was intelligent and cunning enough to be a military spy. The quality of her information—details on troop strength and movements, economic conditions in Richmond, and military strategy—soon changed the general's mind. He and other generals increasingly relied on her to answer their questions about the inner workings of the Confederacy. Sharpe later testified that the greatest amount of information he received from the Confederate capital in the winter of 1864–65, "in its collection, and in a good measure in its transmission, we owed to the intelligence and devotion of Miss E. L. Van Lew."[22]

Secret Codes

To ensure the privacy of the messages he and Van Lew exchanged, Sharpe asked that she use a secret code which he provided. Van Lew copied the key to the code onto a two-inch scrap of paper, then hid it behind a photograph inside an ornate watch which she wore at all times on a chain around her neck. Any notes or messages she received were concealed in a hollow figurine on her mantel during the day. At night she kept them on a lamp stand beside her bed, ready to be burned should the need arise.

Even if her messages were masked in code, there was great danger in getting them into and out of Richmond. In the beginning, Van Lew was naive enough to simply send letters by mail. As the war progressed, however, she turned to more surreptitious means. She tore coded papers into pieces, then rolled them into tiny balls which could be hidden almost anywhere and easily overlooked during a search. She sent servants on missions with messages hidden in the soles of their shoes or tucked into an empty eggshell hidden in a basket of eggs. She convinced a seamstress to carry information punched onto tissue paper patterns.

Van Lew's caution was not excessive. She was constantly watched by authorities. "I have turned to speak to a friend and found a detective at my elbow. Strange faces could be seen peeping around the column and pillars of the back portico [roofed porch],"[23] she observed. Boarders whom the Van Lews took into their house were asked to report any suspicious activities they saw there. The general in charge of police and prisons even sent one of his men in disguise to the mansion in an attempt to rent a room. Elizabeth felt uneasy about him and turned him away.

From President and Prison

Having a spy in Richmond, capital of the Confederacy, gave the Union an enormous advantage, especially when that spy was as smart and resourceful as Elizabeth Van Lew. Her most audacious scheme was spying on Confederate president Jefferson Davis. One of her servants, Mary Elizabeth Bowser, was an intelligent woman who had been educated at the Quaker School for Negroes in Philadelphia. Instructing her to pretend to be illiterate, Van Lew arranged for Bowser to be hired as a servant in the Davis home.

No record remains of the information Bowser managed to get while she worked at the Davis mansion between 1863 and the end of the war. Undoubtedly it included battle plans and military orders, since Davis was highly involved in the war effort. Thomas Mc-Niven, a Union loyalist who worked with Van Lew in Richmond during the war, remembered, "Mary was the best as she was working right in Davis' home and (she) had a photographic mind. Everything she saw on the Rebel President's desk she could repeat word for word."[24]

Confederate president Jefferson Davis was spied upon by Mary Elizabeth Bowser, a servant of Van Lew.

While Mary Bowser spied in the president's home, Van Lew continued to carry out undercover activities under the nose of authorities in Richmond's prisons. Guards were always eavesdropping on conversations, so Van Lew used silent methods to exchange information with the prisoners. She and the men hid messages in the spines of books that she loaned them. Sometimes they marked pages with simple codes—pinpricks under key words and numbers—that both knew how to decipher. The pricks could only be seen if the page was held up to the light.

Van Lew often carried food into the prisons in an antique French plate warmer—a double-bottomed metal dish in which hot water below warmed whatever sat on top. Many times the pan carried messages rather than hot water, and a prisoner only had to feel the cool metal to know what he had to do. Removing the message, he would quickly write an answer and return it to the pan.

A Clever Disguise

Despite her courage and audacity, Van Lew suffered from being under constant suspicion. Nervous and edgy by nature, she now found herself always casting furtive glances over her shoulder as she walked down the street. Tension made her short-tempered and she gave way to angry outbursts, behavior that no Southern lady was supposed to exhibit.

Finally, she decided to use her nervousness to good advantage. She exaggerated it and began to take on odd mannerisms in public such as humming to herself, holding her head to one side, and having conversations with imaginary friends. She stopped combing her hair, wore a ragged bonnet, and dressed in old, food-stained clothes.

Richmonders had always thought her odd. Soon they decided that she had lost her mind. Children jeered at her and chanted, "Crazy Bet, crazy Bet, lives in a mansion with no rooms to let [rent]."[25] Many people who once suspected her of spying now decided that she was just a harmless, loony "old maid" who didn't deserve their attention.

In 1863, when Confederate general Robert E. Lee ordered that all horses in the South were to be confiscated for use of the Confederate cavalry, Elizabeth did something else that added to her "crazy" reputation. The Van Lews had four white horses to draw their carriage, and three of these were taken. Elizabeth was determined to keep the fourth, since she used it on trips to and from her farm outside town.

Storage sheds and other outbuildings were obvious places to hide a horse, so she opted for the unusual. She directed her servants to spread straw on the floor of her library on the second floor of the mansion. Then they led the animal inside, where it lived until all danger of confiscation was past. "He [the horse] accepted his position and behaved as though he thoroughly understood matters, never stamping loud enough to be heard nor neighing. [He was] a good, loyal horse," Van Lew observed.[26] Neighbors who knew about the horse in the library undoubtedly chalked up the incident as just another example of "Crazy Bet's" bizarre behavior.

Spymaster

In late 1863, Van Lew contacted General Benjamin Butler, a Union commander whose army was stationed near the James River in Virginia, and offered to spy for him. Butler agreed, and the two exchanged messages throughout the war, using secret codes and invisible ink. The information Van Lew provided Butler and other Federal officials included reports on morale in the Confederate army, on high prices and the scarcity of food, on the routes Confederate supply trains took to the battlefield, and other vital facts. One of the messages regarding a possible Union attack illustrates Van Lew's grasp of the facts and the detailed information she supplied:

> No attempt should be made with less than 30,000 cavalry, from 10,000 to 15,000 infantry to support them. . . .

Van Lew hid one of her horses in her house to keep it from being confiscated by the Confederate cavalry.

Forces probably could be called in from five to ten days; 25,000 mostly artillery, . . . [General George E.] Pickett's [brigade] is in or around Petersburg. Three regiments of cavalry disbanded by [Robert E.] Lee for want of horses. . . .[27]

By the third year of the war, Van Lew, whose code name was "Babcock," had recruited a great many people to gather and carry information for her. Her spy ring included servants, businesspeople, and government workers. One Northern official involved in espionage during the war remarked, "They had clerks in the rebel war and navy department in their confidence."[28] Most of these spies were never identified because Van Lew carefully protected those who served with her. The few whose names are known include William White, Lemuel E. Babcock, William Rowley, and a man known only as "Quaker."

None of these agents were professional spies, and the strain of living in enemy territory, trying to appear unsuspicious, and dodging arrest at every turn was surely difficult for them to bear. Many could not even be sure they were safe in their own homes, as Van Lew pointed out in late 1864:

> When the cold wind would blow on the darkest & stormiest night, Union people would visit one another. With shutters closed & curtains pinned together, how have we been startled at the barking of a dog and drawn nearer together, the pallor coming over our faces & the blood rushing to our hearts, as we would perhaps be tracing on a map (General William Tecumseh) Sherman's progress . . . or glorying in our Federal leaders. Then to follow the innocent visitor to the door, to lower the gas as, with muffled face, they said good night & the last words often were, "Do you think I am watched?" Such was our life, such was freedom in the Confederacy.[29]

The End Draws Near

In March 1864, General Ulysses S. Grant became head of all the armies of the Union, and in May he headed south, determined to capture Richmond and bring the war to an end. Now Van Lew's inside information became even more vital. She sent messages regularly to Grant and Butler, including drawings of Confederate defenses around Richmond and Petersburg (a transportation center that Grant besieged in 1864). She revealed the strength of Confederate troops in the region, their movements, and where they were stationed. One such message warned, "The enemy are planting torpedoes [land mines] on all roads leading to the city and fields in front of their line of defenses."[30] Along with her messages, Van Lew thoughtfully included a copy of the Richmond paper and flowers from her garden. Her courier system was so speedy and efficient that the flowers were still fresh when they reached Grant's headquarters.

In June 1864, Grant besieged Lee and his army at Petersburg, and the morale of Richmond residents worsened. Despite the genius and military expertise of Lee, the Confederate army grew weaker and weaker. By April 1865 it could no longer hold off Grant's forces. Petersburg fell into Union hands on April 1, and two days later Richmond did the same. Lee and his troops retreated westward, hoping to regroup and fight again. The war, however, was all but over.

With the news that Confederate forces had left Richmond, a panic broke out in the city. Leaders of the Confederate government including Jefferson Davis left town on the evening train. Other government workers carried boxes of documents into the streets and set them on fire. The fires they started were eclipsed by blazing tobacco warehouses, torched by retreating Confederate troops. Carried on the wind, burning embers set buildings aflame in the business district and beyond. Looters grabbed what they could before it was too late. Homes burned, and families ran helter-skelter into the streets.

Union Flag over Richmond

Although her city was in flames, Van Lew was determined to celebrate the ultimate Union victory. In preparation for the day, she had had a large American flag smuggled into her home. Now she and her servants hurried to the roof and unfurled the banner against the sky. It was the first Union flag to appear in Richmond after the Confederacy fell.

Not surprisingly, her gesture enraged the Richmonders who saw it. A mob formed and people raced up the hill to the Van Lew mansion, intending to tear down the flag or worse. As they neared the house, Van Lew stepped onto the porch. She eyed them defiantly. "I know you, and you!" She stabbed her finger at the crowd. "General Grant will be in town in an hour. You do one thing to my home, and all yours will be burned before noon!"[31] Reluctantly, the crowd broke up.

A short time later Union troops entered the city and put out the fires. Fearing that his chief spy might need protection, General Grant sent a troop of cavalry to Van Lew's home. The men did not find her there. As soon as the fires were out, she had rushed to Confederate headquarters to search for important documents. Her protectors found her sifting through the ashes, looking for anything that might be of value.

A short time later, Grant himself visited Van Lew to thank her for the great service she had done for her country. "You have sent me the most valuable information received from Richmond during the war," he said.[32] The spy was greatly honored by the general's visit, and forever treasured the memory of sitting and drinking tea with him on her spacious porch.

Close to the end of the Civil War, General Ulysses S. Grant (pictured) sent cavalry soldiers to Van Lew's home to protect her.

Outcast

When Richmonders learned the full extent of Van Lew's activities during the war, their hatred for her burned with a fierce and lasting fire. She had spied for the enemy during a time when traitors were abhorred and spies were at the lowest rung on the social ladder. She had helped Union prisoners escape. She had paid workers in the city arsenal to sabotage munitions (weapons). The latter had caused the deaths of many young men, and Southerners viewed such activity as tantamount to murder.

Many could never find it in their hearts to forgive Van Lew for what she had done. She wrote years after the war ended, "I live, and have lived for years, as entirely distinct from the citizens as if I were plague-stricken. Rarely, very rarely is our door-bell ever rung by any but a pauper, or those desiring my service. . . . September (13), 1875 my mother was taken from me by death. We had not friends enough to be pall-bearers."[33]

Not only was Van Lew short on friends after the war, she was also in need of money. Her generous efforts to help the North had used up most of her family's fortune. Grant authorized two thousand dollars to be paid to her as reimbursement for her war expenditures, but that money lasted only until 1867.

Van Lew's financial situation improved from 1868 to 1877. During that period, Grant was President of the United States, and his spymaster, who had been living in poverty, was given the position of postmaster of Richmond with a salary of twelve hundred dollars a year. Richmonders were outraged and insulted by the appointment, and she was subject to much persecution on the job.

Conditions grew worse after Grant left office and she did not have the protection of his patronage. "I am 'hounded down.' The good Lord only knows how bitterly. On account, solely on account of my principles & having stood firmly—but quietly by them," she wrote to President Rutherford B. Hayes's secretary in 1877, asking for help. "There is a terrible conspiracy in my office. This I am forced by my present situation to put up with—my chief clks [clerks] are the leaders."[34]

Despite a satisfactory job performance, without Grant's protection Van Lew lost her post. She was given a position as a clerk in the Washington post office, but that lasted only two years.

Unhappy End

In the last years of her life, Elizabeth Van Lew's personality became one of the greatest handicaps to her happiness and comfort.

As their city lay in ruins, Richmonders hated Van Lew for her betrayal of the South.

She could not understand why Richmonders continued to shun her, and her bewilderment gradually turned to bitterness. Her nervousness and feelings of persecution grew, and she became "troublesome." She would arrive late to church and disrupt the service. She complained that her niece Elizabeth Louise Klapp, who had moved into the mansion to help care for her, was abusive. She wrote letters to newspapers, protesting the government's right to collect taxes from those who had no right to vote. (Women were not given the right to vote until 1920.)

After a lingering illness, Van Lew died in her home on September 25, 1900. She was buried in Shockhoe Cemetery in Richmond, attended by only a few friends. To pay her debts, the furniture, heirlooms, and books that filled her home were sold at auction for less than one thousand dollars. Her collection of personal correspondence with Presidents Grant, Garfield, and Hayes, dozens of Union generals, and authors such as Oliver Wendell Holmes was sold for just ten dollars. The flag she had raised over her home during the fall of Richmond went for seventy-five dollars. Unlike many historic homes that were preserved in Richmond, the Van Lew mansion was torn down in 1911 to make way for a school.

Long overlooked despite her intelligence, daring, and contributions to the war effort, Elizabeth Van Lew was a woman of courage who paid a high price for her principles. Despised by others, she was nevertheless confident that she had made the right choices during a critical time in her nation's history. An entry in her journal makes a fitting epithet:

> If I am entitled to the name of "Spy" because I was in the secret service, I accept it willingly; but it will hereafter have to my mind a high and honorable signification. For my loyalty to my country I have two beautiful names—here I am called, "Traitor," farther North a "spy"—instead of the honored name of "Faithful."[35]

CHAPTER 3

Agent Extraordinaire

Master spy Sidney Reilly was one of the most complex and mysterious secret agents of all time, a shadowy figure who worked for the British secret service during the early 1900s. The embodiment of all that spies are thought to be, he was dashing, romantic, and adventurous and at the same time ruthless, ambitious, and secretive. Biographer Robin Bruce Lockhart observes, "His closest friends described him as 'sinister'; his enemies were forced to acknowledge both his exceptional daring and his compelling charm."[36]

Mysterious Beginnings

The mystery surrounding Reilly, whose given name was Sigmund Georgi Rosenblum, begins at his birth. This is generally accepted to be March 24, 1874, but it could have been 1877. By one account he was born near Odessa, Russia, the only son of Grigory and Pauline Jakovlevich Rosenblum, a wealthy Polish-Jewish couple who owned an estate near the Nieman River. A different account makes him the illegitimate son of Pauline Rosenblum and a Jewish physician. Regardless, Reilly was raised in the well-to-do Rosenblum family. He received an excellent education and showed a remarkable aptitude for languages. He was eventually able to speak seven, including English, Greek, and Russian.

Reilly left home when he was about nineteen as the result of an unhappy love affair. He fell in love with his first cousin, and when the family forbade marriage, the young man cut all ties and set out to seek his fortune.

Several versions exist of the years that followed. He sometimes claimed to have attended a college in India; at other times it was Heidelberg University in Germany. He may have traveled to Brazil where he worked and had many adventures. In one instance he claimed to have saved three British intelligence officers from hostile natives. In gratitude, the officers gave him a British passport that he used to reach Britain.

Some people, though, believe he went straight from Odessa to Britain. Wealthy and with many social connections, the Rosenblum family may have had friends in London who helped him find work. (He claimed to have worked as a chemist at one time, and this would have been that opportunity.) About this time, too, he was approached by British intelligence and recruited as an agent.

Early Intrigues

Reilly was living in Britain and going under the name Sidney Rosenblum when he met and married a well-to-do widow named Margaret Thomas in 1898. He may have been instrumental in murdering Margaret's husband in order to marry her, although no charges were ever brought against him. Shortly after his marriage, he changed his name from Rosenblum to Reilly, his new wife's maiden name. He also became a British citizen.

Dark, handsome, and fastidiously dressed thanks to his wife's money, Reilly appeared to be a prosperous English gentleman. He was described as a "charmer, gregarious, an excellent mixer at all levels, with a reputation as a man who could arrange complex cosmopolitan business deals. . . . All who knew him spoke of his magnetic personality, and his supreme gift of coaxing people to do things for him."[37]

These talents combined with his intelligence and love of danger seem to be the reasons Reilly spied. He loved making a difference in the world in a big way. He loved manipulating others. He loved complexity and intrigue. Even his espionage work was entangled with love affairs and personal business deals that often increased the risks he faced.

Sidney Reilly was born near the city of Odessa, Russia (pictured).

Reilly's espionage career began about 1899, during the Boer War, a conflict between Great Britain and Dutch-descended colonists (Boers) in southern Africa. Reilly posed as a German arms buyer and obtained information for the British on how the Netherlands was getting aid to its allies six thousand miles to the south.

After that successful mission, British intelligence sent him to Port Arthur, a Russian naval base in the Far East, to learn about and report on the growing tension between Russia and Japan. There is evidence that Reilly used his skill and cunning to spy not only for the British but also for the Japanese and the Russians. He provided Britain detailed information on Russian warships, coastal defenses, and dispositions of land troops while accepting large sums of money from the Japanese for the same information. The Russians also paid him to reveal Japanese war plans. Reilly undoubtedly justified his actions with the rationale that his double-dealing did nothing to harm Britain, the country where his ultimate loyalties lay.

New Identities

Returning to Britain about 1904, Reilly enrolled in the Royal School of Mines to study electrical engineering. He graduated

Reilly began his career as a British spy during the Boer War.

with top marks in 1905, then went on to Trinity College, Cambridge, and did research in civil engineering for about two years. Considered an expert in both engineering and spying, his next assignment was in Persia (now Iran). Oil had not yet been discovered in the Middle East, and he was to investigate the possibility of petroleum resources being there.

To mask his real purpose, Reilly pretended to be a patent medicine salesman and traveled by camel from one locale to another, talking, listening, and learning about drilling operations that were under way in the region. When oil was later discovered in the Persian oil fields, he was credited with acquiring them for Britain despite the prior claims of other countries.

As time passed, British intelligence services reorganized and expanded. In 1909 the Secret Service Bureau was formed with Captain Sir Mansfield Cumming as its first chief. Reilly reported to Cumming, but like many espionage agents of the time, he preferred to spy alone rather than as part of a team. He was extremely independent and relied on his quick wit and cool head to get him through dangerous situations. For instance, while on a secret mission to learn about German weaponry prior to World War I, he disguised himself as a welder "with cropped hair, roughened grimy hands, shabby clothes and worn boots"[38] and got a job inside the Krupp armaments plant.

Determined to steal vital blueprints, he strangled a guard and broke into the drawing office. Identifying the plans, he tore them into quarters, sealed them into four envelopes, and mailed them to Cumming in Britain. With the plans safely on their way, he managed to escape with the Germans hot on his heels.

Russian Schemes

Reilly's next assignment was to learn everything he could about German naval power for the British. To that end, he formulated another audacious plan. The Russian government was preparing to rebuild its navy and poised to hire a German shipbuilding company—Blohm and Voss—to do the job. Pretending to be Russian, Reilly went to St. Petersburg where, with the help of a government official named Massino in the Ministry of Marine, he got a job as a Blohm and Voss sales representative. He was handsomely paid by the company for the many contracts he obtained for them, and, as part of his job, all blueprints for new Russian ships—patterned after Germany's own warships—passed through his hands.

Getting the prints to Britain remained a problem, but Reilly was up to the challenge. Working behind locked doors at night, he spent hours making copies of each print. The originals went to

After getting a sales job with a German shipbuilding company, Reilly sent Russian warship plans to the British.

Russia's Minister of Marine; the copies were sent to Britain. Lockhart writes, "His duplicity was completely successful. For three vital years before the outbreak of the First World War, the British Admiralty were kept up to date with every new design or modification in the German fleet—tonnages, speeds, armament, crew and every detail even down to cooking equipment."[39]

Not only did Reilly steal warship designs, he also stole Massino's wife, Nadine, marrying her in New York about 1916. Reilly was still married to his first wife, Margaret, but because he wanted to be with Nadine, he had persuaded Margaret to disappear out of his life by using a combination of threats and bribes.

Behind the Lines

The years during World War I are largely unaccounted for as far as Reilly's spying is concerned. This was in great part because Reilly himself preferred to keep his undercover activities secret, both for his own safety and in order to remain a nameless, faceless entity. He liked to quote a Russian proverb that said, "The cow that makes the most noise gives the least milk."[40]

Nevertheless, there are a few accounts of his work during this period. Some may be exaggerated versions of the truth or even outright fabrications. However, Reilly undoubtedly engaged in secret missions during the war, and the results of his work completely satisfied the secret service.

On several occasions he was dropped into Germany and Belgium by plane to gain information for the British on German troop dispositions. Because he spoke German like a native, he could pretend to be a farmer or businessman and get away with any masquerade. Sometimes he posed as a German soldier. Once he actually enlisted in the German army as a private and sent messages to Cumming by carrier pigeon. Reilly was promoted to a commissioned rank in the German army before he managed to slip away.

In the most daring exploit of all, Reilly pretended to be the chief of staff of Rupert, the prince of Bavaria. As such he was able to attend a planning conference with the German high command which included Kaiser Wilhelm, emperor of Germany. There, according to Lockhart, "Reilly learnt of the plans for the massive U-boat onslaught on British shipping which nearly won the war for Germany in 1917. Thanks to him the British Admiralty were forewarned."[41]

Revolution in Russia

In early 1917, while World War I was still raging, an event occurred in Russia that would significantly impact the remainder of Reilly's life and career. Public demonstrations and strikes—triggered by war, a battered economy, and Czar Nicholas II's oppressive regime—led to nationwide revolution and the overthrow of the government. Months of turbulent conditions followed until the Bolshevik (Communist) Party, headed by Vladimir Lenin, gradually consolidated its power and took control of the country. Shortly thereafter, Lenin switched allegiances (Czar Nicholas had been allied with Britain) and signed a peace treaty with Germany, Britain's enemy.

In Britain, Prime Minister David Lloyd George was naturally wary of the Bolsheviks, who opposed democracy and capitalism. More important, he was concerned because Russia was now out of the war. More than a million German soldiers who had been fighting on the Russian front were now free to go up against the British on the Western Front. Thus, Lloyd George directed Cumming to put his best agent on the job to learn of Lenin's intentions. He also wanted Russia to return to the fight against Germany if that could be managed.

Cumming chose Reilly for the Russian assignment. The master spy was a unique personality—independent, temperamental, and unpredictable. His ideas and lifestyle were grandiose. He was a gambler and a womanizer. He was totally unscrupulous when it served his purposes. But he was also immensely talented and had numerous contacts in Russia that could serve him well.

Recruited for what was possibly the most important mission of his life, Reilly set out. This time his heart was fully in his work because he hated the Communists, describing them as cowardly ruffians and archenemies of the human race.

After Vladimir Lenin (pictured) took control of Russia, the British assigned Reilly to obtain information about Lenin's intentions.

Cumming had given Reilly a virtually free hand to do what needed to be done to accomplish his goals; so from the first, his plans were unexpected and daring. Trying a direct approach, he marched into the Kremlin (offices of the Soviet government) and demanded to see Lenin, intending to ask him point-blank what Bolshevik intentions were. That tactic failed, so Reilly resorted to more devious means of gathering intelligence.

Assuming several identities—among them, a Greek named Constantine and a Russian named Massino—he traveled between St. Petersburg (renamed Petrograd) and Moscow, making contacts, gathering information, and testing loyalties. He managed to obtain the identity papers of a member of the Russian secret police, and these allowed him to move about and question people at will. He set up a network of agents among dissatisfied army officers. In Moscow, he moved in with a dancer and two young actresses who agreed to work for him. Lockhart writes, "It was not long before Reilly's sexual magnetism began to have its effect on this female trio. Soon there was little they would not do for Reilly and his cause. During his assignment in Russia, Reilly amassed a number of mistresses whose help to him was invaluable."[42]

A Personal Cause

Exactly when Reilly decided to overthrow the new Russian government is unclear. It is also unclear whether Cumming and Lloyd George totally approved of his activities in that regard. Certainly they would have preferred to see the Bolsheviks unseated and a government more friendly to the West in power, but they were not ready to publicly endorse assassination or a coup d'état (the overthrow of the government).

Reilly was, however. Meeting with leading counterrevolutionaries in Moscow, he helped put together a scheme to depose the Bolsheviks and replace them with men of his own choosing. He later claimed that he had the support and services of sixty thousand Russian and Latvian soldiers who had been loyal to the czar and were easily bribed.

Before Reilly's plan could be finalized, however, the Russian secret police got word of it and went after the conspirators. With sweeping speed they made a number of arrests, including eight of Reilly's mistresses. One British diplomat was killed and thousands of suspected enemies of the state were executed. A reward was issued for Reilly, his description was printed in newspapers and on posters throughout the country, and the secret police were instructed to shoot him on sight. However, a fellow spy in Russia finally managed to obtain false identification papers for Reilly and helped him escape to safety.

A trial was held in Moscow shortly after the attempted coup and Reilly was condemned to death in absentia (while not present) for conspiring against Lenin and the Communist regime. Apparently honored by the attention, Reilly wrote to an acquaintance in October 1918, "The Bolsheviks have done me a great honour. . . . They have put a great price on my poor head. I can boast of being 'the most sought after man' in Russia."[43] In Britain, the master spy was shortly thereafter awarded the Military Cross for his dangerous exploits.

Reilly attempted to overthrow the Bolsheviks by gathering sixty thousand soldiers who were loyal to Czar Nicholas II (pictured).

The Trust

Reilly could not return to the Soviet Union, but he was still determined to overthrow the Bolsheviks. He continued to spy for Britain, but he focused most of his energy on strengthening anticommunist movements. In 1923 he took time out from international intriguing to divorce Nadine and marry a beautiful South American actress—Pepita Bobadilla. It was his second bigamous marriage because he had never divorced Margaret Thomas.

While Reilly worked to defeat his enemies, they plotted to crush him. Soviet intelligence officials created an allegedly anticommunist organization called the Monarchist Union of Central Russia, also known as The Trust. The Trust attracted people who were opposed to the Bolsheviks and wanted to overthrow them. Soviet intelligence secretly controlled the organization, however, and its true aim became identifying and eliminating anticommunists in and outside Russia.

Believing that The Trust had the money and means to make great changes in Russia, Reilly set up a meeting with its representatives in 1925. He was fully aware that the organization might be a Communist front, yet he did not want to reject any possible means of weakening the Soviet government.

Moving cautiously, he ascertained that The Trust representatives he was scheduled to meet were reliable and above suspicion. Because he was still a wanted man in the Soviet Union, he arranged the meeting outside its borders, in the city of Helsinki, Finland. At the September get-together, most of his fears were eased. He was told that "something entirely new, powerful and worthwhile [was] going on in Russia,"[44] and if he wanted to learn more about it he could meet with leaders of The Trust in Moscow. These leaders were so highly placed in government that they could ensure Reilly's safety in the Soviet Union.

Convinced, Reilly agreed. On September 25, 1925, he wrote a letter to Pepita, saying, "I want you to know that I would not

In Britain, Reilly was awarded the Military Cross for his actions in Russia.

have undertaken this trip unless it was absolutely essential, and if I was not convinced that there is *practically* no risk attached to it. . . . I cannot imagine any circumstances under which the Bolshies could tumble to my identity."[45]

The master spy crossed into Russia that night, using a false passport. Unknown to him or the representatives he had met in Helsinki, he had already been betrayed by Trust agents loyal to the Communists. Shortly thereafter, he walked into the arms of Soviet authorities and was never seen by his wife or friends again.

Disappearance

No reliable record exists of Reilly's last days, although most authorities believe he was killed soon after his capture. There are several accounts that confirm this, one of which was printed in the Soviet press. It stated that on the night of September 28, 1925, four "smugglers" were caught crossing the Finnish-Soviet border and that two had been killed. One was so seriously wounded that he soon died, and one was taken prisoner. Reilly was not named, but those who knew of his activities concluded that he was one of the four and probably dead.

Another account states that Reilly successfully traveled to Moscow before being arrested on the orders of Joseph Stalin, who took control of Russia after Lenin died in 1924. There, Reilly was interrogated, perhaps tortured, and revealed information that led to the arrests of a number of his fellow spies and conspirators. Then his captors executed him. Author Michael Kettle describes the scene as he believed it happened. "One morning, while Reilly was taking a walk in the Lenin Hills [a park in Moscow], he was shot in the back by a man named Ibrahim, the OGPU's [Soviet secret police] crack marksman."[46]

Not everyone was convinced that the master spy died in 1925, however. A report in *Izvestia*, a Russian newspaper, stated that Reilly and several members of the Russian nobility were not executed until June 1927. Other reports, unsubstantiated but fascinating, placed him variously in a Russian prison, in America, in the Middle East, and elsewhere up until World War II. "For my part I sincerely believe that he is still alive," Pepita wrote in the foreword of *Britain's Master Spy*, the book she coauthored with Reilly and later published in 1933.[47]

No matter what the truth is, Reilly's death remains as mysterious as his life. He is remembered as an enigma, as a man who had enormous influence on the world during his lifetime, and as one of the greatest spies of history.

CHAPTER 4

The Great Betrayer

One of the highest-ranking British spies of the 1940s and 1950s led a double life that shocked and horrified the West when it discovered the truth. Harold Adrian Russell Philby seemed to be the perfect English gentleman: well born, polished, likable, and patriotic. Yet his loyalty to Britain was a sham. From the time he was a college student, Philby was a devoted Communist working for the Soviet Union. British security expert Sir Robert Mackenzie pointed out, "Philby didn't *sell* his country's secrets. He gave them away. He didn't do it for money. He never got a penny. He did it for his ideals."[48]

Kim

Philby was born in Ambala, India, on January 1, 1912. His father, Harry St. John Philby, was one of many Englishmen who served in India during the era of British colonialization. Well educated and highly intelligent, St. John was a nonconformist and somewhat eccentric. (Later in life he lived in Arabia, became a Muslim, and took a Saudi slave to be his second wife.) In 1910 he married his first wife, Dora Johnston, the red-haired daughter of a railway engineer. Two years later the couple had their only son. Little Harold Adrian was nicknamed Kim after author Rudyard Kipling's famous Indian hero in a book of the same name.

Appearing to be a British loyalist, Kim Philby was actually a Communist working for the Soviet Union.

When Philby reached school age he was sent to England to attend Westminster, a prestigious prep school. In 1929 he entered Trinity College, Cambridge, just as his father had done. The atmosphere at the college felt conservative to him compared to his father's freethinking influence. Philby recalled, "There was in

44

general a stifling atmosphere of closed windows, drawn blinds, expiring candles."[49]

Politically Aware

Philby's political awareness began to develop in 1929. At that time the British government, led by the Labour Party, was failing to deal with the severe economic depression that plagued the country. Philby and a number of other dissatisfied Cambridge students were drawn into the newly created Cambridge University Socialist Society, whose ideology favored radical reform or even revolution to improve society. To Philby, socialism and communism seemed to offer solutions to the economic problems besetting working-class people in Britain. He had only to look to the Communist-led Soviet Union, where the economy seemed to be on a triumphant upswing, to see the contrast between capitalism and communism.

Nevertheless, Philby took his time before rejecting his country's ideology. In 1932 and '33 he traveled to Germany, Hungary, and France, intent on seeing how their societies worked. They, too, were having economic and political problems. In the end it was easy to make a decision. "It was clear to me that other countries were just as bad as Britain and that what I was witnessing was a failure of the capitalist system," he said.[50]

On his last day at Cambridge, in 1933, Philby decided to become a Communist. He later remembered, "I asked a don [professor] I admired, Maurice Dobb, how I should go about it. He gave me an introduction to a communist group in Paris, a perfectly legal and open group. They in turn passed me on to a communist underground organization in Vienna [Austria]."[51]

Going Undercover

In Vienna, Philby made many friends among young Communist and socialist militants. He also married Alice "Litzi" Friedman, a Communist radical who was wanted by the police. The two were in love, but their union served another purpose as well. By marrying Philby, Litzi was able to obtain a British passport and flee the country. The couple returned to London in 1934.

In the mid-1930s, a Communist agent approached Philby and offered him the chance to join the Soviet intelligence service. Philby readily agreed. He was told that his long-term assignment would be to obtain a position in the British secret service. In the short term, Moscow wanted him to get firsthand information on the Spanish Civil War, a struggle between fascists (right-wing nationalists) and Communist forces.

Acting as a journalist in Spain, Philby obtained information for Moscow about the Spanish Civil War.

Opting to cover the war as a journalist, Philby got a job as a reporter for the *Times* of London and set off for Spain. To disguise his true political beliefs, he pretended to be sympathetic to the nationalist cause. So convincing was this masquerade that Francisco Franco, leader of the nationalists, presented him with the Red Cross of Military Merit.

The war ended in 1939 and Philby returned to Britain, intent on developing a new, moderate image. His appearance and manner needed little work. He was slim and good-looking. He could be friendly or aloof, debonair or unkempt, confident or hesitant to suit the situation. He also had a stammer which he could control and use to his advantage when he wanted to appear naive or unsophisticated.

His interests and associations warranted attention, however. He dropped all outward endorsement of Communist principles and led his friends and associates to believe that these had been a result of youthful enthusiasm. He also separated from Litzi so there could be no question that he had cut all ties with his Communist past. Above all things, he wanted to appear to be a loyal British subject.

Moles

With his image renewed, Philby was ready to take the next step to becoming a mole in the British intelligence service. A mole is a double agent who operates against his own government from within its intelligence establishment.

Philby applied for work in Department Six of British intelligence, also known as the Secret Intelligence Service (SIS). (The SIS is so secret that the British government denies all knowledge of it. Officially it does not exist.) It was not hard for Philby to get hired, since the SIS was primarily composed of upper-class men recruited from top-notch universities. Family background was all-important. Little consideration was given to political loyalties. Philby possessed the necessary qualifications, and his father was acquainted with Sir Stewart Menzies, head of the service, so he was accepted without question.

At that time and throughout the 1980s, one of the British secret service's main duties was combating communism. Soviet Communists were the Englishman's bogeymen. Seen as agents of evil bent on taking over the world, they were considered unscrupulous, ruthless, and as much a threat in times of peace as in times of war. Communist spies were thought to be everywhere, and, in fact, this was true to a large extent. The Soviet government, ruling by force and intimidation, recruited agents and planted spies in all parts of the world in order to protect itself and promote its goal of becoming a world leader. Philby was just one example of these efforts, and he was not the only convert from Cambridge. His fellow students Donald Maclean, Anthony Blunt, and Guy Burgess were all recruited as Communist agents during their college years. For decades they—along with Philby—spied for the KGB. Philby, Blunt, and Burgess worked for British intelligence. Maclean worked as a diplomat in the Foreign Office, a government department that deals with foreign affairs and state security.

At the Center of the Service

During World War II, Philby was made head of a subsection of the SIS and helped direct resistance groups and guerrilla activities in German-occupied countries. He did an excellent job in his new position and came away with a reputation of being one of the most promising young agents in the SIS.

In 1944, as World War II drew to a close and hostility increased between the Soviet Union and the West, a new section of the SIS was created to uncover and eliminate any Communist agents who might have infiltrated the British secret service. When Philby told his Soviet control about it, he was directed to do everything he could to become its head. A combination of scheming, office politics, and good luck did the trick. Philby was put in charge of Section Nine, as the new department came to be called.

Donald Maclean, who also went to Cambridge in Britain, was a spy for the KGB.

At first Section Nine was rather small, and focused only on counterespionage. Philby expanded both its size and its mission, however, until he was in charge of all British intelligence and subversion operations against the Soviet Union. Historian and intelligence officer Hugh Trevor-Roper writes, "[Philby] established himself at the very centre of the Service. . . . In secret, how he must have relished that triumph! . . . His Russian masters, too, must have smirked, a complacent, Machiavellian smirk, as they saw their chosen agent moving into this central post."[52]

Philby naturally passed to the Soviets all relevant information he obtained. In his position as head of Section Nine, he was also able to conceal and protect any important Soviet operations against Britain or Britain's allies. The most important secret he kept under wraps, however, was his own allegiance to the KGB.

Near Miss

In 1945, Philby was awarded the Order of the British Empire for the fine intelligence work he had carried out during World War II. Because of his talents and leadership, his fellow workers speculated that he might one day become director of the service. Trevor-Roper writes, "I was convinced . . . that he was destined—and indeed that he was being groomed—to head the Service. . . . Philby was undeniably competent: the most competent and industrious man in that generally lax organization."[53]

That same year, however, Philby's career was almost cut short when Soviet intelligence officer Konstantin Volkov defected to the British embassy in Istanbul, Turkey. Volkov claimed that he could identify Soviet moles in the British government. A report on Volkov was sent to London, and Philby immediately realized that he was one of the moles Volkov intended to name. He quickly alerted his Soviet handler (the case officer he reported to) of the danger, then managed to substitute himself for the intelligence officer that was assigned to interview Volkov in Istanbul.

Philby's plan was to delay the interview in order to give the KGB time to act. It was successful. When he finally arrived in Istanbul and tried to contact Volkov more than a week later, the defector had vanished. Knowing full well that Volkov had been kidnapped and taken back to the Soviet Union to be executed, Philby pretended innocence. He reported to his superior, "The Russians had ample chances of getting on to him. Doubtless both his office and his living quarters were bugged."[54]

Philby's treachery over the years sent many men such as Volkov to their deaths. When later asked if he had regrets for his actions, he replied, "They knew the risks they were running. I was serving the interests of the Soviet Union and those interests required that these men were defeated. To the extent I helped defeat them, even if it caused their deaths, I have no regrets."[55]

New Liaisons, New Assignments

In 1946, Philby married Aileen Furse, with whom he had been living since 1940. The couple had three children out of wedlock, and a baby was on the way when the wedding took place. In order to marry, Philby first had to obtain a divorce from Litzi, who was living in East Berlin with a known Soviet agent. This brought her to the attention of the SIS, who also learned that she had spied for the Soviets while she was living in Britain before the war. Despite Philby's past ties to someone with so dubious a reputation, he was not seen as a security risk and was able to continue his work as a British agent and a mole.

In 1947, Philby was sent to Istanbul. There he worked for the British, cleverly managing operations so that several anticommunist groups were betrayed and sent to their deaths.

Two years later he moved to Washington, D.C., to be a liaison officer between the SIS and the Central Intelligence Agency (CIA). This placed him at the very heart of the most vital Western espionage operations. While in Washington, Philby was able to pass to the Soviets secrets about American long-term military intentions, relations between America and its allies, the status of its atomic research, and covert U.S. intelligence operations to be mounted against the Communists. In some cases he learned information so top secret that the Soviets could not use it. If they

While working in Washington, D.C., Philby informed the Soviets of American military plans.

had, Philby would have come under instant suspicion because he would have been one of only a few who could have leaked it.

Exposure

In late 1950, while Philby was in Washington, D.C., he learned that his old college acquaintance Donald Maclean, who held an important position in the British embassy in that city, was in danger of being exposed as a Soviet spy. Maclean, who was a heavy drinker, had become careless in his espionage activities for the Soviets and attracted the suspicion of the CIA and SIS.

Philby alerted the KGB to Maclean's danger but could not directly warn Maclean, who was in London at the time. The danger of drawing suspicion to himself was too great. Philby did notify Guy Burgess, however. Burgess was a flamboyant and somewhat reckless agent who served at the British embassy and was a close friend of Maclean. Burgess immediately flew to London and alerted Maclean, even though the action brought Burgess himself under suspicion.

There was only one way the two men could save themselves. On the day that Maclean was to be interrogated by the SIS, he and Burgess fled to Moscow. Their defections—unspoken admissions that they were Soviet spies—appalled and outraged British and American intelligence agencies. Neither group wanted to believe that they had harbored traitors in their midst. Philby himself did his best to appear disbelieving. "[I took] the line that it was almost inconceivable that anyone like Burgess, who courted the limelight instead of avoiding it, and was generally notorious for indiscretion, could have been a secret agent, let alone a Soviet agent from whom strictest security standards would be required. . . . Of Maclean, I disclaimed all knowledge."[56]

A Bold Front

Because of his long friendship with Burgess (Burgess had even lived with the Philbys for a time in 1950), Philby quickly came under suspicion of being in alliance with the Soviets. This was no surprise to him. He had already buried the camera and other equipment he used to copy documents in a lonely wooded area some distance from his home. Confident that there was no concrete proof to convict him, he decided to remain calm and see what the future would bring. He later wrote, "I was guided by the consideration that unless my chances of survival were minimal my clear duty was to fight it out. [There might yet be] an opportunity for further service."[57]

Philby's decision brought him to the brink of disaster, but not ruin. The CIA decided that he was no longer welcome as a liaison officer in America, and he was recalled to London shortly after the Maclean-Burgess scandal. There he faced an investigation of his career—including his Communist leanings during college, his marriage to Litzi, his work in Spain, the Volkov affair, and his affiliation with Burgess. At least one man, Dick White, a senior officer in British intelligence, concluded from that investigation that Philby was a Soviet spy. "I have totted up the ledger and the debits outweigh the assets," White stated.[58]

There was much discussion in British newspapers that Philby was the third man in the so-called Cambridge Spy Ring, a circle of spies that included Burgess and Maclean. (The Cambridge Spy Ring eventually proved to be real and much larger than originally supposed. It also included Anthony Blunt and John Cairncross, both of whom worked for British intelligence and spied for the Soviets.) Philby put up a bold front, however. He resolutely denied that he was a spy and protested that he was being accused solely because of his friendship with Burgess and his connection with Maclean in college. Some people believed him. Others did not.

In the end, investigators could not prove that Philby was guilty, but his reputation was so tarnished that he was asked to resign. Despite the dismissal, the head of SIS, Sir Hugh Sinclair, helped Philby get a job as a journalist/correspondent for two British periodicals, *The Observer* and *The Economist*.

Oddly enough, the SIS reemployed Philby shortly after his dismissal. (Some experts believe that he never left the service in the first place.) The reasons he was reestablished are not clear. Perhaps his superiors wanted to keep an eye on him in order to await further developments. Perhaps they did not want to admit to themselves and others that they had unwittingly employed another Soviet spy, especially one so highly placed in the service. At any rate, Philby remained a member of the SIS until 1963.

Philby claimed that he was being investigated simply because of his friendship with Guy Burgess (pictured).

He also conscientiously maintained his espionage work for the Soviets. Because he no longer had a top position inside the service, however, most of his reports were simply political observations rather than intelligence information.

Crisis

In December 1957, while Philby was stationed in Beirut, Lebanon, his wife, Aileen, died of heart problems. Philby was having an affair with Eleanor Brewer, wife of a *New York Times* correspondent, at the time and, in 1958, Brewer divorced her husband to marry Philby.

A peaceful married existence was not in the cards for Philby, however. In December 1961, KGB officer Anatoli Golitsyn defected to the CIA and gave information that positively identified Philby as a Soviet spy. A new investigation began, and by the end of 1962 the SIS was convinced of Philby's guilt.

When confronted, Philby admitted that he had spied and appeared willing to give a full confession of all his activities. However, on January 23, 1963, in a torrential rainstorm, he boarded a cargo ship bound for Russia, leaving his wife and children behind. Of his defection he said, "I knew exactly how to handle it. God knows I

52

had rehearsed it often enough. Just a little stalling, just a little drinking to show nothing was afoot, just a little time to make assurances along the escape route doubly sure. Then, at a given signal, away and gone! How could they have stopped me?"[59]

A New Life

His spying days at an end, Philby spent the rest of his life in the Soviet Union, becoming a Soviet citizen, learning Russian, and being made a KGB general. Disastrously for the West, he gave the Soviets every detail of British and American intelligence material he had ever gleaned. Biographer Phillip Knightley writes,

> He named every officer he had ever met or knew about, every agent ever employed, every operation ever mounted. He described how each service was organized, who reported to whom and how, and the physical layout of all the service buildings. . . . Nothing was considered too insignificant or trivial to be recalled and recorded.[60]

It took decades to assess the damage Philby did to the West both before and after his defection. When asked if he had regrets about such a devastating betrayal, he replied, "To betray, you must first belong. I never belonged."[61]

In late 1963, Eleanor Philby joined her husband behind the Iron Curtain. The couple lived in a comfortable five-room apartment in Moscow, were provided with a maid and a chauffeur, and

After defecting to the Soviet Union, Philby worked as a general in KGB headquarters (pictured).

had access to a country home when they wanted to get away from the city. It was a life of luxury by Soviet standards, but for Eleanor the cold weather, monotonous existence, and lack of consumer goods were extremely irritating.

In 1965, after learning that Philby was having an affair with Donald Maclean's wife, Eleanor returned to the United States. She died there in 1968. In 1971, Philby married his fourth wife, Rufina Ivanova, a woman twenty years his junior. He later said, "I made up my mind twenty seconds after meeting Rufa that she was the woman I wanted to marry."[62]

Death in Moscow

Philby continued to work for the KGB, analyzing intelligence operations and giving motivational lectures. He received many awards, although he was proudest of the prestigious Order of Lenin that he received in 1965. "It's the equivalent of a K(knighthood), you know," he explained. "Of course there are different sorts of Ks, but the Order of Lenin is equivalent to one of the better ones."[63]

Kim Philby died on May 11, 1988, of heart disease and was buried with full military honors in Kuntsevo Cemetery in Moscow. In 1990 the Soviet government issued a postage stamp in his honor, citing him as a KGB hero. In the Western countries he had betrayed and then renounced, however, few were generous enough to speak words of admiration and forgiveness. Richard Helms, former CIA director, expressed a widely held point of view. "He was a traitor to his country and the free world. I do not shed any crocodile [false] tears over his demise. I don't know that the damage that he did can ever be actually calculated."[64]

CHAPTER 5

Undercover at Pearl Harbor

On March 27, 1941, the Japanese ocean liner *Nitta Maru* slid up to Pier 8 in Honolulu Harbor, Hawaii, and its passengers prepared to disembark. One of the last to leave was a young diplomat, vice-consul Tadashi Morimura. Although he held a relatively unimportant position, Morimura was welcomed ashore by the consul general himself. Wearing a welcoming lei, Morimura was conducted through customs, then driven to the Japanese consulate. There he was given his own cottage on the grounds, a luxury that most of the staff did not enjoy.

Morimura's fellow workers soon learned that he had other privileges as well. He earned a generous salary but worked any hours he wished. Sometimes he came into the office at 11 A.M. and left by 1 P.M. His lack of skill on the job was obvious to everyone, yet his superiors never criticized him. Most of the staff guessed that he had connections with some powerful person in Japan who had helped get him a job in the popular, tropical setting.

Ensign Takeo Yoshikawa

Morimura did have a powerful sponsor, Captain Kanji Ogawa, head of naval intelligence in Japan. The young vice-consul's real name was Takeo Yoshikawa, and he was not a diplomat but a spy, sent to learn everything he could about military forces in the U.S. territory of Hawaii.

Born March 7, 1914, on Shikoku Island, Japan, Yoshikawa was the son of a policeman and grew up believing in the virtues of self-discipline, sacrifice, and absolute loyalty to one's country. Both at home and at school he was taught the military arts, and became a champion at *kendo*—stick fighting—a sport popular in the armed forces. He could also swim eight miles through rough seas.

After leaving middle school, Yoshikawa was accepted into the Imperial Japanese Naval Academy. He graduated in 1933, then served at sea for a brief time. In 1934, however, he developed a

Takeo Yoshikawa was sent to Pearl Harbor, Hawaii, to learn about American military forces there.

severe stomach ailment, and two years later was discharged from the navy. His career apparently had reached an early end. "My retirement was a great shock, since all my plans and hopes were bound up with the Navy," he wrote.[65]

Assignment: Spy

Yoshikawa's retirement was not permanent, however. In 1936, a Japanese naval intelligence officer approached him and asked if he would be interested in joining the Third Bureau, the naval general staff's intelligence group. Yoshikawa eagerly accepted. He was told to improve his English and become an expert on the U.S. Pacific Fleet and the American naval bases at Guam, Manila, and Pearl Harbor, Hawaii. The U.S. military was blocking Japan's quest to expand its power in the Pacific, and the tiny island nation planned to go to war, if necessary, to achieve its aims. Before that could happen, however, it needed to know everything it could about its enemy. "I read a vast amount of material in that period, from obscure American newspapers to military and scientific journals devoted to my area of interest," Yoshikawa later explained.[66]

When he passed his English-language exams, Yoshikawa was given his assignment. Masquerading as a member of the consulate, he was to go to Hawaii and uncover the strength and readiness of American military forces there. He was not given the reason for his assignment, although he guessed his country's intentions. His superior made it clear that he was to carry out operations in the most secret manner possible. Japanese consul general Nagao Kita was the only other person in Hawaii to know the spy's true identity. Kita had been instructed to cooperate with and support Yoshikawa in every possible way. Yoshikawa later remembered that he was honored and pleased by the assignment. "In my heart I rejoiced," he said.[67]

Investigating Oahu

Yoshikawa was not familiar with the islands when he arrived in Hawaii in March 1941. In fact, he later recalled that the only useful information he initially possessed was the fact that the Seaview Inn served an excellent balloon-fish soup. He made it his business to learn quickly, however.

First he focused on the naval base at Pearl Harbor, heart of the U.S. military presence in the islands. The enormous shamrock-shaped basin with a narrow channel opening to the sea was a strategic locale because it was home to virtually the entire U.S. Pacific Fleet. Heavy cruisers, submarines, battleships, destroyers, and aircraft carriers all came and went from "Pearl" regularly. Thousands of naval personnel were stationed there to maintain, refit, provision, and operate the vessels. Journalist John Vandercook wrote in mid-1941, "Pearl Harbor is one of the greatest, if not the very greatest, maritime fortresses in the world. It is one sure sanctuary in the whole of the vast Pacific, both for ships and men. Hawaii's seas and cliffs guard not only it, but the hemisphere behind it."[68]

Because the naval base and surroundings were off-limits to most civilians, Yoshikawa had to find vantage points from which he could observe the harbor. His favorite became the Shuncho-ro, a Japanese-style teahouse located in Alewa Heights, just north of Honolulu. It had a sweeping view of Pearl Harbor with the naval air station on Ford Island in the center, the navy shipyard, arsenal, oil depot, and Hickam Airfield on the east side, and dozens of ships moored in the East Loch and surrounding area.

Yoshikawa discovered that the restaurant even had a telescope on the second floor to make his observation easier. He later remembered:

In the early 1940s, Pearl Harbor housed most of the U.S. Pacific Fleet and thousands of naval personnel.

On many nights, after I made my preliminary observations, I would wind up at the *Shuncho-ro* in a little Japanese-style room, grateful to be sitting on the rice-straw *tatami* mats again and talking once more with a *geisha*. I never disclosed my identity or purpose to the functionaries at the restaurant, but always insisted on a room with a view of the harbor. At nights, with the lights blazing, it was a magnificent sight indeed, and at first light, when the sorties [outbound operations] usually began, I could gain much useful information on ships present and deployment patterns.[69]

Under Suspicion

Almost everything that Yoshikawa wanted to learn about the U.S. Pacific Fleet and its workings was out in the open and easy to see. Airfields, harbors, and ships were clearly visible to anyone who climbed the island's mountain slopes and looked down.

The spy knew, however, that even innocent activities would be suspect if they were carried out by a Japanese. The U.S military was highly suspicious of the thousands of Japanese who had immigrated to Hawaii over the years. Military officials were convinced that many retained their loyalty to Japan and would do all they could to further its interests.

Thus, the military kept the Japanese sampan fleet (fishing and freight boats) away from the entrance to Pearl Harbor and allowed few Japanese to work at the various airfields, the navy yard, or the munitions and fuel depots. U.S. authorities were constantly looking for signs of espionage, especially at the Japanese consulate. Consul General Kita was always under close surveillance, other members of the staff were watched, and consulate phones were tapped.

Knowing that he was suspect, Yoshikawa took ample precautions. He was always careful to be inconspicuous. When he walked through the cane fields that overlooked the harbor, he dressed as a laborer. When he drove to Pearl City north of the harbor and walked out on a pier, he dressed casually, wore different clothing each time, and always limited his trips to two or three a week. If he thought he might be noticed, he left the area and returned another day at another time.

Whenever possible, Yoshikawa posed as a tourist, carrying an island map and a camera slung over his shoulder as props. He never used the latter, however, preferring to commit to memory what he saw. He seldom used binoculars either. Even when he discovered that boat tours of the Pearl Harbor base were available for tourists, he decided not to take advantage of the opportunity to view the ships and installations at close range. The fear of

To avoid discovery, Yoshikawa disguised himself as a laborer when walking through sugar cane fields.

somehow drawing attention to himself and his activities weighed constantly on his mind.

"Bobby Make-Believe"

To further negate any suspicions directed at him because of his job as vice-consul, Yoshikawa went one step further and adopted a careless, playboy lifestyle that hid his true character. He privately called this persona "Bobby Make-Believe." "Bobby" not only ignored his work at the consulate, he hung around restaurants and bars, drank too much, and stayed up late. He hosted noisy *sake* (rice wine) parties at his cottage. He flirted outrageously with all the women he met. Sometimes he dated a Japanese-American schoolteacher; at other times he wrote love poems to a geisha who worked at a Honolulu teahouse. In general, he cultivated the reputation of being thoughtless and unreliable.

The deception worked. Those who monitored Japanese activities on Hawaii routinely judged Yoshikawa to be the most harmless of individuals. His name never appeared on any of the FBI's lists of dangerous persons.

Innocent Tourist

With his cover as a carefree bachelor firmly in place, Yoshikawa expanded his explorations. He took sightseeing trips, methodically explored Oahu's roads and back roads, and identified every point of military interest. Sometimes he went swimming on beaches around the island, searching for potential landing sites for invasion forces. In May he invited two women from the consulate on a boating excursion on the east side of Oahu. One of the boat's attractions was a glass bottom that allowed passengers to view the ocean floor. Yoshikawa was able to check the depth of the water in Kaneohe Bay, and soon thereafter reported to his superiors that the bay was too shallow for large ships to anchor there.

In early autumn Yoshikawa decided to undertake air reconnaissance, and made several tourist sightseeing flights over Oahu. The thirty-minute trips allowed him to see the number and direction of runways at Wheeler Airfield, count the number of hangars at Wheeler and Hickam Airfields (from which he estimated the number of planes each would hold), and confirm the accuracy of earlier ground-level observations he had made.

A few weeks later he went on a three-day trip to the big island of Hawaii. In his role as innocent sightseer he stayed at a tourist hotel in the city of Hilo, purchased postcards, visited waterfalls, and hiked to a volcano. At the end of his visit he had formed a mental picture of Hilo harbor and could report on the construction of a new airport on the Kapu Military Reservation. His hike to the volcano allowed him to view a Hawaiian National Guard camp.

Painstaking Procedures

Yoshikawa could have turned to informants and Japanese sympathizers to assist him in his espionage, but he chose to work alone for a number of reasons. First, he knew that the more people who knew about his activities, the greater the risk of exposure. Second, he was somewhat disdainful of local Japanese, judging them to be careless, unreliable, and unimaginative. Finally, he found that most of the Japanese population in Hawaii—particularly second-generation Japanese born in Hawaii—were loyal to the United States. He later stated that "those men of influence and character who might have assisted me in my secret mission were unanimously unco-operative."[70]

Cautious and always on guard, Yoshikawa never carried anything that would incriminate him if he were stopped by authorities. He waited until he returned to his cottage on the consul grounds to record his observations. There, he kept all notes and codebooks locked in a room that his maid was never allowed to clean.

On a trip to the big island of Hawaii, Yoshikawa stayed at a tourist hotel to conceal his real intentions.

Information that he noted, coded, and sent to Japan at least twice monthly conformed to Captain Ogawa's preference for facts and figures rather than impressions and opinions. Thus, Yoshikawa made sure he included both numbers and names of ships in his reports. One typical message read: "Battleships eleven: *Colorado, West Virginia, California, Idaho, Mississippi, New Mexico, Pennsylvania, Arizona, Oklahoma, Nevada,* and *Utah.* Six heavy cruisers. Ten light cruisers. Thirty-seven destroyers. Eleven submarines. The airplane carrier *Lexington*, with two destroyers, is cruising off the east shore of Oahu island."[71]

Yoshikawa also reported that few patrols, air or otherwise, were conducted north of Oahu. Battleships were moored in pairs in Pearl Harbor, and the ones closest to shore were not vulnerable to torpedo attack. He noted that most ships were in harbor on the weekends and that their crews were on leave at that time. Crews did not seem to be on the alert for a possible attack, ships were not camouflaged in any way, and no barrage balloons were visible in any locale. (Barrage balloons were huge balloons sometimes anchored around military sites. Wires or nets hung from them and provided protection against attack by low-flying aircraft.)

Because the information he wrote down was so incriminating, Yoshikawa was careful to hide exactly what he was doing even from other members of the consul staff. The code room at the embassy had barred windows, and the door was lined with heavy

Twice a month, Yoshikawa sent messages to Japan regarding the names and numbers of American ships.

sheet metal. Yoshikawa sent his cables to Japan using Honolulu's four cable companies. He alternated his use of each to mask the routing of the messages. The messages themselves were addressed to the foreign minister in Japan and signed by Consul General Kita so as to appear to be diplomatic communications. In fact, the foreign minister never saw them. Instead they were delivered to Captain Ogawa, who passed them on to Admiral Isoroku Yamamoto, head of the Japanese Combined Fleet. In Hawaii, Kita passed Ogawa's messages directly to Yoshikawa.

Cracked Code

Despite all their caution, Yoshikawa and his superiors did not realize that the United States had successfully cracked the codes they were using. The many incriminating messages that Yoshikawa sent to Japan were readily available for his enemies to read. Fortunately for the Japanese, however, the lag between receipt and decoding was sometimes quite long. For instance, Yoshikawa's December 6, 1941, message—"I imagine that in all probability there is considerable opportunity left to take advantage for a surprise attack against these places [Pearl Harbor, Hickam, Ford, and Ewa]"[72]—could have alerted the Americans to Japan's intentions. The message was not decoded and read for the first time until December 8, though, a day after the Japanese attacked Pearl Harbor. A similar delay occurred in reading many of the final cables that passed between Hawaii and Tokyo in late November and early December 1941. Even when these intercepted cables were read in time, they were not taken seriously because few Americans believed that tiny Japan would dare attack a world power such as the United States.

"Very Urgent"

On September 24, 1941—less than three months before the bombing of Pearl Harbor—Consul General Kita received a message for Yoshikawa marked "very urgent." The Pearl Harbor spy discovered that his work needed to become even more detailed than before. Captain Ogawa directed him to divide a map of Pearl Harbor into grids; then he was to report the presence of U.S. ships in each grid section.

Always conscientious, Yoshikawa went one step further. He subdivided the grids and established his own designations. The east side of Ford Island he called section FGA, the west side of the island FGB, the repair dock in the navy yard KS, a region near Ford Island FV, and the navy dock in the navy yard KT. On

September 28, using his new plotting scheme for the first time, he sent a report. It read:

(1) FGA—one *Texas*-class battleship, total one.
(2) FGB—one *Indianapolis*-class cruiser, one unidentified-type heavy cruiser, total two.
(3) FVBC—seven light cruisers of *Honolulu*- and *Omaha*-class; 26 destroyers.
(4) KS—one *Omaha*-class light cruiser.
(5) Also, six submarines, one troopship, and two destroyers off Waikiki.[73]

East Wind, Rain

As the weeks passed, Yoshikawa was asked to report more often. Between November 18 and December 6 he sent twenty-four telegrams to Japan. Although he was never told exactly when the attack on Pearl Harbor would occur, he was not surprised to hear a distant rumbling about eight o'clock on the morning of December 7, 1941. "I thought it probably a maneuver, but rose and switched on the short-wave [radio],"[74] he recalled. Twice in the course of the broadcast on Radio Tokyo he heard the announcer say, "East wind, rain," a code that war with the United States had begun. (The code phrase "North wind, cloudy" would have meant war with Russia; "West wind, clear" meant war with Britain.)

The Japanese had put Yoshikawa's information to good use. That morning, almost 360 Japanese planes attacked Pearl Harbor and the airfields at Hickam, Bellows, Wheeler, Ewa, and Kaneohe. In the course of the attack, which lasted more than two hours, bombers and torpedo planes hit ships, naval personnel, and civilians. Eight American battleships and thirteen other naval vessels were sunk or severely damaged. Fortunately for the United States, the aircraft carrier *Lexington* had left Hawaii on December 5 for a cruise into southern waters and thus avoided the attack.

Almost two hundred American aircraft were destroyed in the early-morning surprise raid. Three thousand military personnel were killed or wounded. As a result of the strikes, President Franklin Roosevelt declared war on Japan, and the United States entered World War II against the Axis powers (Germany, Italy, and Japan).

Finale

Yoshikawa had little time to exult in his success. He and other consul members realized that all Japanese persons in Hawaii would soon face investigation if not imprisonment, so they quickly began burning their codebooks and other incriminating papers. Many letters and documents had been destroyed earlier in the year, so the job was virtually complete by the time police arrived. Ironically, the officers were sent to the consulate not to make arrests, but to protect the staff and property from angry Americans seeking revenge.

The FBI soon arrived to search the premises, however. Yoshikawa was detained with the rest of the staff for ten days. He was later transported to an internment camp in the United States. Eventually he was sent back to Japan, where he continued to work in naval intelligence until the end of the war. When American troops occupied Japan in 1945, he fled to the countryside for fear that he would be killed if his true identity became known. It was 1960 before he revealed himself and his past to the American public.

Takeo Yoshikawa was one of many spies who worked in Hawaii prior to World War II, but he was undoubtedly the leading espionage agent on the islands at that time. The quality and quantity of information he gathered and reported proved invaluable to the Japanese as they planned their attack on Pearl Harbor.

During the attack on Pearl Harbor, twenty-one naval ships and vessels were sunk or damaged, and three thousand military personnel were killed or wounded.

Yoshikawa died in Japan in 1993. No other event in his life ever measured up to his period of service in Hawaii. He stated in a rare 1960 interview,

> I am older now, and dwelling more in the past as the years go by. Some things certainly are ordained. And so it was that I, who was reared as a naval officer, never came to serve in action, but look back on my single top-secret assignment as the *raison d'etre* [justification] of the long years of training in my youth and early manhood. In truth, if only for a moment in time, I held history in the palm of my hand.[75]

CHAPTER 6

Atomic Bomb Spies

In 1950, Julius and Ethel Rosenberg seemed to be an unremarkable young married couple, raising a family in one of New York City's working-class neighborhoods. Two years later they were convicted spies, two of the most controversial of the twentieth century. People around the world argued over whether they were traitors to their country or victims of a government witch-hunt. Presidents, the pope, and Supreme Court justices gave opinions regarding the Rosenbergs' guilt and punishment. For decades it seemed that the truth would never be known. Then in the 1990s, new evidence came to light and the dispute was settled once and for all.

Serious and Mournful

One of the primary participants in the Rosenberg case, Esther Ethel Greenglass, was born on September 28, 1915, in a section of New York City known as the Lower East Side. Her parents, Barnet and Tessie Greenglass, were a poor Jewish couple who lived directly behind the family business, a small sewing machine repair shop. Ethel was a serious, idealistic child with a mournful face and a high, sweet singing voice. She dreamed of singing professionally when she grew up. Her practical-minded mother despised her ambitions, however, and refused to pay for music lessons. "If God had meant for Ethel to have music lessons, he would have provided them," Tessie Greenglass said.[76]

After graduating from high school, Ethel put aside her dreams and became a secretary at a freight company that packaged and shipped clothing. In her spare time she took part in union activities associated with her work and in left-wing (socialist and Communist) political events. Her involvement in the latter was not considered terribly scandalous because the 1930s were a time of pro-leftist feeling in the United States. Hitler and his right-wing Nazi Party posed an increasing threat to Europe, and the Communist-led Soviet Union was America's ally. There were plenty of young Americans who believed that the Soviets' experiment with communism should be supported and encouraged.

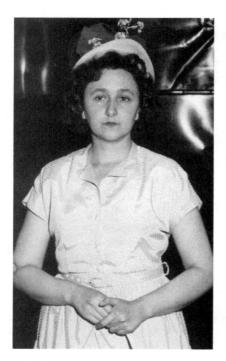

Because she enjoyed performing, Ethel sang whenever she could at the political rallies and benefits she attended. At a fund-raising rally in December 1936, a young college student named Julius Rosenberg heard her and complimented her on her talent. For both it was love at first sight. Ethel saw the intellectual Julius as her "savior" from an unhappy family life. She did not hesitate to marry him when he proposed in June 1939.

Young Communists

Julius Rosenberg was born in New York City on May 12, 1918, to Harry and Sophie Rosenberg, Jewish immigrants from Poland. Like the Greenglasses, the Rosenbergs were poor and lived on the Lower

Ethel Rosenberg's interest in communism began during the 1930s.

East Side. Harry was a tailor and Sophie a homemaker. "I remember we were so poor my mother hard-boiled the eggs, so she could divide one among us," Julius's older sister recalled.[77] For a time Julius studied to become a rabbi, then decided to attend City College in New York (CCNY) where he majored in electrical engineering.

CCNY was a center of radical political activity in New York. Many of its students identified with Communist and socialist ideals, and some of its professors were Communist Party members. Julius, interested in socialism and communism from his high school days, became wrapped up in political activities. "Julie [Julius] loved to talk of 'the new world, the future, Socialism.' And he talked of it not as an abstraction or some world far removed. . . . It was always in immediate terms, living and vital, as if it were just over the horizon," recalled a friend.[78]

A number of Julius's friends and acquaintances at CCNY were interested in communism, too. Morton Sobell, William Perl, and Joel Barr were engineering majors and part of the Steinmetz Society, a radical engineering group to which Julius also belonged.

"People like me were attracted to communism because it seemed to offer a rational explanation for what was wrong with society. Capitalism wasn't rational," Morton Sobell explained later.[79]

Home and Family

Julius graduated from CCNY in 1939, the same year he married Ethel and officially became a member of the Communist Party. Whether Ethel joined the party is unclear, but she shared her husband's political beliefs and attended party meetings regularly.

In 1940, Julius found civilian work with the Army Signal Corps, where he inspected electronic equipment designed for the U.S. armed forces. His outspoken enthusiasm for communism soon aroused concerns at work, however. "He was not always cautious," one friend reported. "I think he sold the *Daily Worker* [a Communist newspaper] or at least introduced it to some of his fellow workers. [He] shot off his mouth."[80] Despite his open loyalty to communism, Julius denied a connection to the Communist Party when the Signal Corps questioned him about it in 1941.

Once Julius had a good job, Ethel quit working and became a traditional homemaker. In 1943, a son, Michael, was born to the couple and in 1947, Robert came along. Ethel's health deteriorated after her pregnancies, but she continued to loyally support Julius's commitment to communism.

In 1939, Julius Rosenberg graduated from college, married Ethel, and officially joined the Communist Party.

Calculated Risks

In 1943, Julius withdrew his membership from the Communist Party, stopped his subscription to the *Daily Worker*, and became less involved in party activities. He explained the change by claiming he wanted to spend more time with his family. However, distancing oneself from the party

Soldiers work with proximity fuses, a device that Julius Rosenberg sold for the Russians.

was a common move for people who became spies for the Soviet Union. They wanted to have no overt ties to communism if they came under investigation.

Such proved to be the case with the Rosenbergs. Julius had been recruited as a spy in 1942. His work with the Signal Corps gave him access to developments in the field of radio electronics, and these he passed on to his case officer and contact, Alexander Feklisov. Feklisov, a KGB officer, posed as a diplomat in the Soviet consulate in New York City.

Julius met with Feklisov at least fifty times between 1943 and 1946. At one meeting Rosenberg arrived with a large box containing a proximity fuse, a device used to bring down enemy aircraft. He had smuggled it out of work. "I have a Christmas present for the Red Army," he announced proudly. When he was criticized for taking unnecessary risks, he replied, "I calculated the risks very carefully. What I was risking was only one-hundredth of what a Red Army [Soviet] soldier risks when he attacks a tank."[81]

Spy Ring

Because Julius was friends with other young men who had Communist leanings, he was able to convince them to spy for the Soviets. At the end of 1942 he persuaded Joel Barr, who worked at Western Electric in New York City, to supply Feklisov with classified information on radar systems. Julius and Barr then recruited a friend, Alfred Sarant, who helped Barr photograph a variety of secret documents. A KGB report revealed that Barr alone supplied "217 authentic drawings [pertaining to a] high-resolution airborne radar system."[82]

Barr and Sarant were not Julius's only recruits. William Perl, who worked for the National Advisory Committee for Aeronautics, agreed to provide the Soviets important information on aeronautics. The data that he handed over was used in the manufacture of Russian MiG fighter planes used in the Korean War. Morton Sobell, who worked at General Electric, provided information on military radar systems and future radio engineering projects.

Atomic Secrets

In 1943, Ethel Rosenberg's younger brother, David Greenglass, was inducted into the U.S. Army. Like his sister Ethel, David was a Communist sympathizer. So was his wife, Ruth. The following year he was sent to Los Alamos, New Mexico, where he became one of many scientists, technicians, and machinists who worked on the Manhattan Project, the development of the atomic bomb. As a machinist, David did not have top security clearance on the project, but he was on-site daily and knew a great deal about what was going on.

When Julius discovered the nature of David's work, he asked him to "share it" with the Soviets. David agreed. He described his decision to spy for the Soviets as "like the feeling one has before plunging into a cold lake."[83] Nevertheless, he and Ruth were committed. Before they returned to New Mexico, David gave Julius some notes and sketches of a high-explosive lens mold he had seen at Los Alamos. Julius gave David and Ruth a recognition token—one-half of a panel from a Jell-O box. He told them that someone bearing the other half of the box would approach them, and they should turn over further information about the atomic bomb to him.

On June 3, 1945, a courier made contact with the Greenglasses in New Mexico. The courier's name was Harry Gold, although the only identification he gave David was the Jell-O panel and a password greeting. Gold, a short, dumpy man and a chemist by profession, was prone to lie whenever it suited him. Nevertheless, he was an effective courier. Anatoli Yatskov (alias Yakovlev), the Soviet officer in charge of atomic espionage in the United States, used Gold to pick up secret information from several sources including spy Klaus Fuchs, a top-level British physicist who was also working on the Manhattan Project.

In 1945 the Greenglasses met Gold several times in New Mexico. The information they supplied included names of scientists who worked on the Manhattan Project, descriptions of the Los Alamos complex, and a description of the atomic bomb that was dropped on Nagasaki at the end of World War II.

Cold War

By the mid-1940s, relations between the Soviet Union and the United States had changed dramatically for the worse. Soviet premier Joseph Stalin's brutal government policies, which resulted in the starvation or execution of millions of his own people, and his use of the Soviet Army to control much of Eastern Europe caused Americans to view communism with mistrust and disapproval.

After the United States pledged to fight the spread of communism under the Truman Doctrine of 1947, hostilities between the Soviet Union and the West developed into a Cold War, with the threat of nuclear conflict looming on the horizon like a black cloud. Assistant Attorney General O. John Rogge announced in November 1947 that the Department of Justice was planning "a dramatic round-up of dozens of Communist leaders and alleged fellow-travellers [Communist sympathizers]"[84] within the United States. As a result the Communist Party of America went underground. It was no longer safe or acceptable to be left-wing.

David Greenglass's commitment to communism and spying changed as time passed, too. In 1946 he was discharged from the

The West feared nuclear attack if the Soviets learned the secret of the atom bomb.

army and returned to New York City. He and Ruth just wanted to settle down, raise a family, and get ahead in life.

The Rosenbergs, however, remained loyal to the party, and Julius continued his espionage work. He had been fired from the Signal Corps in 1945 as a result of his prior Communist affiliation, but had gotten work at the Emerson Radio Corporation. In 1946 he, David, and two other men became partners in the G & R Engineering Company. The business did not do well, however, and tension developed between the brothers-in-law. Julius accused David of being slipshod in his duties. David claimed that Julius spent too much time with his "secret work."[85]

Danger Looms

Then in 1949, danger loomed for the two families. After intercepting and decoding secret Soviet intelligence messages, the United States learned that Klaus Fuchs was working for the Soviet Union. When challenged, Fuchs admitted that he had given away secret information about the atomic bomb, developed while he was working on the Manhattan Project.

In his confession, Fuchs stated that he had turned over his secrets to a courier known as "Raymond." Raymond was a short man with dark hair. He was an American. With a combination of persistence,

Klaus Fuchs admitted that while working on the Manhattan Project he had passed on atomic bomb information to the Soviets.

a description of the courier, and a list of suspicious individuals from whom to choose, the FBI soon determined that Raymond was Harry Gold. When confronted, Gold confessed and named "a soldier, non-commissioned, married, no children (name not recalled)"[86] as another contact who had given him information about the Manhattan Project.

Again the FBI had to puzzle out the unknown's identity, but in the end they managed to come up with a name and photographs. Gold identified David Greenglass, saying, "This is the man I contacted in Albuquerque, New Mexico, in June, 1945."[87]

When Julius and Ethel Rosenberg read about Klaus Fuchs's confession in the newspaper, they realized its implications for themselves and the Greenglasses. In case they would need to flee the country, Julius closed his checking account, redeemed the few savings bonds he and Ethel held, and had passport photos taken. He also warned his brother-in-law that he and Ruth were in danger and advised them to obtain passports as well. Julius even offered David several thousand dollars for travel expenses (allegedly provided by the Soviets). David, however, refused to believe that he was in danger and took no steps to save himself or Ruth.

He realized his mistake, however, when FBI agents arrived to question him on June 15, 1950. The agents emphasized that there was no use denying anything; Harry Gold had identified David as providing top secret documents to the Soviets. Frightened, David signed a confession stating that he and Ruth had been asked to engage in espionage by Julius Rosenberg. Some people believed David Greenglass implicated his brother-in-law out of resentment or simply as a result of pressure from the FBI. He insisted that such was not the case. "They didn't put pressure on me," he later said. "I said I gotta make a choice. This (indicating Ruth who sat beside him) gotta stay with me. They (the Rosenbergs) gotta take care of themselves."[88]

Arrest and Trial

On July 17, 1950, the FBI arrested Julius Rosenberg and charged him with spying for the Soviets. Ethel was arrested on August 11. There was no real evidence to prove that she had helped her husband spy, but the FBI felt that by putting pressure on her they could make Julius confess. Both of the Rosenbergs denied any involvement in espionage throughout their entire seven months in prison, where they awaited trial.

In March 1951 the Rosenbergs went on trial in New York City before Judge Irving Kaufman. Morton Sobell was tried with them. (Other members of the spy ring either fled the country or were tried separately.) The three were tried under the Espionage Act of 1917, which made spying for a foreign country illegal and established severe penalties for such activities.

During the trial, both David and Ruth Greenglass testified for the prosecution in order to reduce David's prison sentence. Their time on the stand was highly damaging to the Rosenbergs. David stated clearly that he had passed secret information about the atomic bomb to the Soviets at the request of Julius. Ruth provided testimony about Ethel's knowledge of and involvement in her husband's activities, stating that on at least one occasion Ethel had typed secret information that David had given to Julius. "[Ethel said] that all his time and energies were used in this thing [spying]; that was the most important thing in the world to him."[89]

When Harry Gold took the stand, his direct link to the Greenglasses and to Anatoli Yatskov, a Soviet spy, was compelling evidence to the jury that espionage had in fact taken place. Gold also emphasized the Rosenbergs' guilt by testifying that the name "Julius" had come up twice in conversations he had had with the Greenglasses.

More Harm Than Good

When Julius and Ethel went on the stand, their testimony and demeanor were as damaging to their case as the prosecution witnesses had been. Julius firmly denied that he had ever been disloyal to the United States, but took the Fifth Amendment (the right against self-incrimination) when asked if he had been a member of the Communist Party. His self-righteous, superior attitude, stony expression, and inept explanations of the Greenglasses accusations turned the jury against him from the start.

Ethel's testimony was equally injurious. She was cold, unemotional, and terse in her statements. She continually took the Fifth

David Greenglass provided damaging testimony about the Rosenbergs during their trial.

Amendment even in answer to questions that would not have incriminated her. For instance, when asked if she had ever helped her brother join the Communist Party, she refused to answer even though David Greenglass had never been a member of the party, and she could have validly denied involvement. Under cross-examination she became hostile. Some members of the jury became convinced that she was the brains behind the spy ring, a point never alleged by the prosecution.

The Lawyers

The Rosenbergs' lawyers hurt their clients' case as well. Emanuel "Manny" Bloch, an attorney sympathetic to Communist ideals who frequently in court defended leftists, led the defense, but from the beginning he underestimated the seriousness of the Rosenberg case. He did not take into account the anticommunist hysteria gripping the United States in the early 1950s or the fact that the Rosenbergs' connection to the Communist Party would be a serious strike against them. Also, he had no plan to counter the anticommunist hatred expressed by prosecuting attorney Irving Saypol and the vigor with which he would attack the Rosenbergs.

From the beginning of the trial Bloch was unnerved by Saypol's forceful manner. As a consequence he failed to make points that would have supported his clients' innocence. Unwittingly, he even hurt their cause. When David Greenglass began to testify about the material he had given to Harry Gold, Bloch insisted that details be suppressed, claiming that it would be better for national security if they remained secret. "I was not at all sure in my own mind whether or not even at this late date, this information might not be used to the advantage of a foreign power," he stated.[90] Bloch had good intentions, but he inadvertently supported the prosecution's arguments that the Rosenbergs had given the secret of the atomic bomb to the enemy.

The Jury Deliberates

On March 28, 1951, the jury retired to determine the guilt or innocence of the Rosenbergs. The twelve—one woman, eleven men; one black, eleven white—had listened carefully throughout the trial. They had disliked David Greenglass but concluded that he spoke the truth, since it was unlikely that he would make up testimony against his own sister. They were unsympathetic to the Rosenbergs. And they were impressed by the fact that even Manny Bloch believed that important national security secrets had been stolen. Now they were ready to vote their consciences.

All twelve voted to convict Julius and Morton Sobell. Eleven voted to convict Ethel. The lone dissenter, James Gibbons, was a religious man who believed she was guilty, but was reluctant to sentence a mother with two young children to possible execution. His fellow jurors finally convinced him to change his vote by asking if he were willing to risk Ethel being free to spy again. "What if she takes part in a conspiracy that dooms *your* children?" they pointed out.[91] Gibbons relented, and when the jury returned to the courtroom they found all three defendants guilty as charged.

Death Sentence

On April 5, 1951, Judge Kaufman sentenced the Rosenbergs to die in the electric chair. Persons as influential as J. Edgar Hoover, head of the FBI, believed that Ethel's death sentence was wrong. Hoover warned that it would generate "a psychological reaction (on the part) of the public"[92] that would reflect badly on the justice system of the United States. Kaufman, however, believed that the Rosenbergs had done worse than murder, and their actions warranted the ultimate punishment. He said to them:

> Your conduct in putting into the hands of the Russians the A-bomb years before our best scientists predicted Russia would perfect the bomb has already caused, in my opinion, the Communist aggression in Korea, with the resultant casualties exceeding 50,000 and who knows but that millions more of innocent people may pay the price of your treason. Indeed, by your betrayal you undoubtedly have altered the course of history to the disadvantage of our country.[93]

Kaufman then sentenced Morton Sobell to thirty years in prison, explaining that his espionage activities were less serious

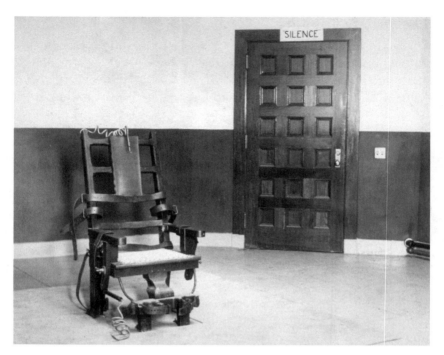

In 1951, the Rosenbergs were sentenced to death in the electric chair.

than the Rosenbergs'. David Greenglass earned a fifteen-year prison term, and Ruth was never tried at all.

The Rosenbergs had expected Julius's sentence to be harsh, but they were unprepared for Ethel's condemnation. Visibly shaken, they returned to their separate cells to await transportation to the "Death House" at Sing Sing Prison, in Ossining, New York. In order to help encourage her husband, Ethel spent the evening singing operatic arias and popular songs such as "Goodnight, Irene." Julius responded with a rendition of "The Battle Hymn of the Republic."

Appeals and World Opinion

The Rosenbergs' death sentence was not carried out immediately. As Hoover had foreseen, a portion of public opinion turned against the Justice Department, especially after it was revealed that some of the prosecution witnesses were suspect, that the defense had been weak, and that Judge Kaufman had appeared biased at times. A number of people began to believe that the Rosenbergs were innocent and had been framed. Others simply felt that they had not received a fair trial. In November 1951 the National Committee to Secure Justice in the Rosenberg Case (known as the Rosenberg Committee) was formed with the aim of letting the world know about the injustice of the verdict. The committee hoped to pressure the government into holding a new trial.

In part due to the efforts of the Communist Party, outcry against the verdict soon spread worldwide. Nobel Prize–winning physicists Albert Einstein and Harold Urey petitioned for clemency. The governments of France, Great Britain, and Italy as well as Pope Pius XII asked the United States to show mercy to the couple.

In the United States, Manny Bloch continued to fight for his clients. Twice he appealed for a new trial, but both times his appeals were denied. On January 11, 1953, President Harry Truman was presented with a petition for executive clemency, which he refused to grant. One month later, newly inaugurated president Dwight D. Eisenhower was also petitioned. He, too, rejected the request.

The Supreme Court Decides

On June 17, 1953, just two days before the executions were scheduled to take place, an event occurred that had the potential to save the Rosenbergs. Tennessee lawyer Fyke Farmer had researched the case and come to the conclusion that the two had been tried under the wrong law. The Espionage Act of 1917 had been replaced by the Atomic Energy Act of 1946. The later law did not allow the death penalty to be imposed unless a jury recommended it. In the Rosenberg case, Judge Kaufman alone had determined that the couple should die.

Despite Bloch's strong resistance to any outside help, Farmer took his arguments to the Supreme Court. Only one of the justices, William O. Douglas, was available for a meeting, but he agreed that Farmer might have a valid point. He granted a stay of execution until the entire Court could consider the matter.

The Rosenbergs rejoiced when they heard of the stay. Their joy was short-lived, however. When the Court met on June 19, the justices determined that the executions should take place that evening. That afternoon, Ethel wrote a final letter to her children. "Only this morning it looked like we might be together again after all. Now that this cannot be, I want so much for you to know all that I have come to know. Unfortunately, I may write only a few simple words; the rest your own lives must teach you, even as mine taught me."[94]

Execution

Just after 8:00 P.M. on June 19, 1953, Julius Rosenberg was escorted into the black-and-white-walled execution chamber at Sing

Sing and strapped into the electric chair. A minute later the executioner pulled the lever. At 8:06 a doctor pronounced the prisoner dead, and his body was removed.

Ethel followed. Julius had been pale and shaky, but she appeared composed and calm. After being strapped into place, three powerful jolts of electricity were sent through her body. The doctor then checked for a heartbeat and was dumbfounded to discover that she was still alive. Two more shocks followed, and at 8:16 P.M. she, too, was gone. Ethel Rosenberg was the first woman to be executed for a federal offense in the United States since Mary Surratt was hanged in 1865 for her part in Lincoln's assassination. The Rosenbergs were the only spies ever to be executed in peacetime America.

Julius and Ethel Rosenberg were buried in Wellwood Cemetery on Long Island, where a crowd of one thousand gathered to mourn their passing. Most Americans, however, believed that justice had been done, that the Rosenbergs had gotten what they deserved. "Americans who betray their country . . . must expect the consequences of their acts," stated the *Philadelphia Tribune*.[95]

Settling the Controversy

Time passed, but the Rosenberg case remained controversial. Books and articles were written arguing the couple's innocence or guilt. Since both of them had gone to their deaths without confessing, it seemed likely that the truth would always remain in shadow.

Many mourners attended the Rosenbergs' funeral on Long Island.

Then in 1995 the Venona files—top secret Soviet diplomatic documents that identified dozens of Soviet agents working in the United States during the 1940s—were released by the U.S. government. In them, proof of the Rosenbergs' guilt was revealed. Julius Rosenberg (code name "Liberal") was referred to numerous times, and even the depth of Ethel's involvement was spelled out. A November 1944 memo spoke of "liberal's wife," whose last name was "that of her husband, first name Ethel, 29 years old." She was described as a party member who "knows about her husband's work," but "in view of delicate health does not work."[96] Another memo mentioned the recruitment of Ruth Greenglass, whom "liberal and his wife recommend . . . as an intelligent and clever girl."[97]

In 1997, Alexander Feklisov also spoke out, confirming his relationship with Julius Rosenberg and the information the spy ring had supplied the Soviets. The Venona files and Feklisov removed all doubt of Julius's guilt, but they also proved that Ethel was involved only to the point of supporting her husband's work. She had not been the brains behind the spy ring as some had alleged.

Looking Back

The Rosenbergs represented much that is reprehensible to Americans. They were disloyal to their country and disdainful of their fellow citizens. Despite their treachery, however, most people who look back at the case agree that they did not deserve to die. The information they gave the Soviets was damaging to America, but not as damaging as was alleged. They did not give away the secret of the atomic bomb; the material David Greenglass passed was sketchy and full of inaccuracies. In fact, Klaus Fuchs passed detailed information about the bomb to the Soviets in June 1945, before David began spying in earnest. Even if David's information had been accurate, it would only have confirmed what the Soviets already knew.

In different circumstances the irregularities of the Rosenbergs' trial, the shortcomings of their attorneys, and the weakness of the evidence against them would have earned them a new trial. They undoubtedly would have been sentenced to a term of imprisonment, but not to death. As it was, their ends were unnecessarily tragic due to misguided loyalties and anticommunist hysteria that gripped America in the aftermath of World War II. As authors Ronald Radosh and Joyce Milton point out, "The fate of the Rosenbergs remains a blot on America's conscience."[98]

CHAPTER 7

CIA Mole

When top-level CIA operative Aldrich Ames was arrested by the FBI in 1995, America learned that he was one of the most dangerous and destructive secret agents ever to spy against the United States. Ames was mediocre on the job, a failure in his personal life, and sloppy in his traitorous activities. Yet he sent men to their deaths and eluded capture for years. A coworker who helped catch Ames says, "What did Rick Ames ever achieve? What was he successful at? Was there anything? . . . He was only successful in one area—betraying other people."[99]

Small-Town Boy

Aldrich Hazen "Rick" Ames was born on May 26, 1941, in River Falls, Wisconsin, a small town located about twenty-five miles from Minneapolis/St. Paul, Minnesota. He was the only son of Carleton and Rachel Ames. Carleton was a professor at River Falls Teachers' College; Rachel taught high school English.

When Rick was eleven his father was offered a job with the Central Intelligence Agency (CIA). Carleton had written a doctoral thesis on Burma's struggle for independence, and the CIA saw him as an expert on that country. He could move there and pose as an academic while gathering information about Burmese politicians and military leaders. The family moved to Burma (now Myanmar) in 1953, but Carleton proved a failure as a spy. Nevertheless, when the family moved back to the United States in 1955, he continued to work as an analyst for the agency in Washington, D.C.

Rick Ames spied for the Soviets

Rick was a mediocre student in high school—"I'd procrastinate and I was lazy," he said[100]—but he was intelligent enough to became a National Merit Test semifinalist. Although he looked like a nerd with thick glasses and a skinny body, he was voted "Most Witty" in his class and performed in several class musicals and dramas. He pursued an acting career for a time after graduation, then decided to become a CIA agent. Due to his father's connections, in 1967 he was accepted into the agency's Junior Officer Training program.

First Assignments

After training, Ames's first assignment was in Ankara, Turkey, where he was to recruit new spies for the CIA. He took along his wife, Nancy, whom he married in 1969. On the job, Ames proved to be like his father, good at writing reports and performing other routine analytical tasks, but terrible at recruiting. He was too reserved, too unattractive, a little odd. He had a great deal of confidence, however, and did not seem aware that his arrogant attitude and grubby appearance annoyed his fellow workers. "He was really, well, just unkempt. His hair in particular was hanging down to his shoulders and I swear he just cut it with scissors by himself. . . . He had these old glasses that were clearly out of style. He had bad teeth and he smoked all the time," recalls one female CIA agent.[101]

Recalled from Turkey in 1972, Ames was given a desk job at CIA headquarters in Langley, Virginia, where he continued to excel at paperwork. After four years of building his reputation, he was promoted and given the job of recruiting Soviet officials living in the United States. He worked out of New York City.

Although he remained ineffective as a recruiter, Ames did become a competent handler for two Soviet informants, Arkady Shevchenko, undersecretary general of the United Nations, and Sergey Fedorenko, a lower-level UN diplomat. Shevchenko supplied secret information about Soviet arms programs, economics, and a feud between Leonid Brezhnev, general secretary of the Soviet Communist Party, and Aleksey Kosygin, premier of the Soviet government. Fedorenko provided data on missiles, KGB agents, and the Soviet defense industry.

Disillusionment

About 1976, Fedorenko was recalled to the Soviet Union, and in 1978, Shevchenko defected to the United States. That left Ames with no agents to handle. He was assigned to be case officer to

After being recalled from an assignment in Turkey, Ames took a desk job at CIA headquarters in Virginia.

another Soviet but was not satisfied with the work. He felt his superiors were not appreciating him.

In addition, over time he had begun to wonder about the CIA. Its work did not seem to be producing results that were important to America. He explained,

> By the late Seventies, I had come to question the value of a great deal of what we were doing . . . and to question whether this was having any significant impact on American policy. . . . I found that, for example . . . our Soviet espionage efforts had virtually never, or had very seldom, produced any worthwhile political or economic intelligence on the Soviet Union.[102]

A welcome change for Ames was in the works, however. In 1981 he was sent to Mexico City, a top meeting place for KGB agents and U.S. spies. Shortly thereafter he was promoted to a rank reserved for senior employees in the agency. "It had taken me forever to get my other grade promotions in New York City, and here I was suddenly being promoted the first time I was eligible. I thought, *Hey, I am still competitive in my career after all.*"[103]

Masquerading as a diplomat in the State Department, Ames was assigned to keep an eye on Cuban and Soviet espionage activity. His cover allowed him to have a generous expense account for entertaining. It also opened doors for him to attend formal dinners, receptions, and cocktail parties. Ames had become a heavy drinker in New York, but now his drinking moved to a new level. He remembers, "I began taking long lunches with my colleagues, and I was getting drunk alone at night in my apartment at least once or twice every week. Of course, by this time, people were beginning to notice, and I was getting a reputation for overdoing it in social settings, but no one really said much."[104]

Rosario

Nancy refused to leave New York when Ames went to Mexico. Their marriage was falling apart, and she had a job and friends in the city. Ames did not regret her choice. He dated other women, then discovered a new passion—Maria del Rosario Casas Dupuy. Rosario, as she was known, was Colombian, a cultural attaché at the Colombian embassy in Mexico City. She was also on the CIA payroll, although her work consisted only of passing on bits of information she heard during parties and allowing her apartment to be used occasionally for secret meetings.

Agents were discouraged from becoming involved with foreign nationals and CIA informants, but Rick didn't care. He and Rosario began an affair. Ames was enthralled with his new love. Rosario came from a prominent family in Colombia. "My mother likes to call us 'impoverished aristocrats,'" she said.[105] She was intelligent, sophisticated, sexy, and beautiful. Ames did everything he could to please her, including buying her clothes and jewelry and taking her to expensive restaurants and exotic getaways.

Rosario loved both the luxury and the attention. She was shocked, however, when Ames revealed to her that he worked for the CIA. "I kept thinking, 'This can't be true. I fell in love with a diplomat, not a spy!'"[106]

Open Doors

In 1983, Ames was reassigned to CIA headquarters in the United States. He was made branch chief of Soviet counterintelligence operations. He was given access to all of the CIA's most sensitive information including the names of agents and double agents in the Soviet Union and details of CIA operations in the Soviet Union.

Ames also learned the names of Soviets working for the CIA in the United States. Two were Sergey Motorin and Valery F. Martynov, assigned to the Soviet embassy in Washington. It was no longer his job to serve as case officer to agents such as these, however. He was supposed to study and devise ways to improve CIA operations as well as come up with new ways to protect CIA agents. It was an interesting and exciting job, and Ames was pleased that he had been given the chance to do it.

In 1983, Ames learned the names of two Soviets who were spying for the CIA at the Soviet Embassy in Washington, D.C. (pictured).

Money Problems

When Ames moved back to the United States, Rosario came with him. She was excited about living "the good life" in America, although she was openly disdainful of American culture and constantly compared it unfavorably with the South American way of life. Her continual criticism had its effect on Ames, and the loyalty he felt for his country gradually faded.

The couple planned to marry, but first Ames had to get a divorce. In accordance with CIA requirements, Rosario also had to become a citizen. She balked at that because of her feelings about America, but finally took the necessary classes and passed the naturalization test with a perfect score. Later she told Ames, "I don't care what I say when I raise my hand or what papers I sign. I'm not an American and I will never be one and no ceremony will change that."[107]

While the couple waited for Ames's divorce to become final, Rosario spent money as if they were wealthy. Ames could not afford her extravagance, but was afraid if he asked her to cut down, she would leave him. He took out a small loan and applied for more credit cards, but those were only temporary solutions. By late 1984 he faced bills that totaled more than thirty-five thousand dollars. His annual salary was less than seventy thousand.

Feeling particularly desperate on the way home from work one evening, he toyed with the idea of getting a second job. Then he thought of robbing a bank. By the time he reached home, however, he had come up with the definitive solution. He knew of at least one case where a CIA agent had been offered fifty thousand dollars by the Soviets to become a double agent. Ames realized that he could turn traitor and his troubles would be over. He states, referring to his disillusionment with the CIA and America itself:

> A lot of barriers that should have stopped me from betraying my country were gone. I also had come to believe that the CIA was morally corrupt. No, my feelings were more intense than this. I had come to believe that it was a dangerous institution. The CIA is all about maintaining and expanding American imperial power, which I had come to think was wrong.[108]

"The Perfect Scam"

On April 16, 1985, after having several double vodkas to bolster his courage, Ames boldly walked into the Soviet embassy in New York and presented them with a sealed envelope. Inside was a page from a CIA directory with his name highlighted, a brief history of his CIA service, and the names of three CIA spies. In return for the names, Ames demanded fifty thousand dollars.

According to Ames, the names he sold were those of three Soviets who were purportedly spying for the United States. The CIA had learned from an overseas contact, however, that these men were in fact still loyal to the USSR. Ames remembers, "I thought, *Gosh, I could tell the KGB about these three cases and demand fifty thousand dollars. The KGB would have to pay me, because if it didn't it would be admitting that these were double agents. So I'd get my money without really harming anyone because these weren't real traitors.* It was the perfect scam."[109]

According to Soviet intelligence chief Viktor Cherkashin, however, Ames's letter did not name double agents planted by the KGB, but true agents that the Soviet Union had not known about. Two of the names were Sergey Motorin and Valery Martynov, whom Ames had first learned about in 1983. "This act, by itself, convinced us that he was a senior CIA officer, because we knew only a few officials would be told the names of spies in our embassy," Cherkashin states.[110] Both Motorin and Martynov were called back to the Soviet Union, where they were arrested and executed.

Treachery on a Grand Scale

Once Ames began his career as a mole, he did not stop. He continued to access the names of Soviet agents working for the United States, carried them out of the CIA in a briefcase or shopping bag, and then delivered them to the KGB in exchange for money.

Passing the documents involved the utmost secrecy. Ames and his contact used "dead drops," such as crevices under bridges or in hollow trees. Ames wrapped the documents in plastic and hid them at a specified drop site, then placed a chalk mark on a particular mailbox or wall to let his contact know what he had done. The contact later drove to the drop site and replaced the documents with a package of money. Ames would know that he could pick up his money when the mark on the mailbox had been erased.

From 1985 to 1994, Ames spied for the Soviets, betraying more than one hundred covert U.S. intelligence operations and more than twenty Soviet agents who were working for the United States. At least ten of those agents were arrested and executed by the KGB.

One of the men Ames betrayed was Sergey Fedorenko, the agent he had handled and become friends with during the 1970s. Another loss—more devastating for the CIA—was Major General Dimitri Polyakov, a Soviet intelligence officer who had spied for the United States for nearly twenty years. Due to his high rank, Polyakov had been able to provide a vast amount of valuable information on chemical and biological warfare, nuclear strategy, Soviet missiles, and other political-military matters. After years of risk, he had retired and was enjoying life with his grandchildren when Ames gave him away. "It should have gone down in history as the greatest spy story of all time," says one CIA agent. "Unfortunately Rick Ames decided to write another ending to that story."[111]

Big Spender

Unlike other spies who worked out of principle, Ames always demanded that he be well paid by the Soviets. Between 1985 and 1993 he received payments of cash and stocks and was promised the titles to property in Russia. The total came to more than $2.5

million, $1 million of which Ames deposited in banks in the United States, Colombia, and Switzerland.

As his income increased, so did his spending. After he and Rosario were married on August 10, 1985, they paid cash for an expensive home in an exclusive Washington, D.C., suburb. They bought new furniture and cars and purchased property in Colombia. Ames got his teeth capped. Rosario enjoyed shopping for designer clothes and fine jewelry. She spent $25,000 taking college classes. She spent almost $30,000 in long-distance phone calls to her mother in Colombia. She and Ames also charged more than half a million dollars on various credit cards between 1985 and 1993.

Despite all the money, Rosario was not satisfied. A son, Paul, was born in November 1988, but caring for him seemed an enormous burden. She constantly criticized Ames for not paying

Major General Dimitri Polyakov, a spy for the United States, provided the Americans with information about Soviet missiles and nuclear strategy.

enough attention to her. She nagged, got angry, and insulted him and their friends. Ames did all he could to avoid her lengthy scoldings. "A number of times when we went to lunch, Rick would get wasted [drunk], and then he would say, 'Please don't tell your wife that you were out with me, because I don't want her to tell Rosario because of all the trouble it will cause at home," a coworker remembered.[112]

What's Happening?

Ames's personal habits were just one example of his recklessness. For a man whose professional success depended on caution and attention to detail, he was extraordinarily careless. As early as 1975 he thoughtlessly left a briefcase containing information about a Soviet double agent on a New York subway car where it could have fallen into the wrong hands. After becoming a mole, he openly carried secret information out of his office despite the serious repercussions he would face if caught. Once he was late to a rendezvous point and missed his Soviet contact. He made mistakes on dead drops, using white crayon (instead of chalk) on mailboxes that his contact could not remove quickly. "Do not repeat," was his handler's response to that mistake.[113]

CIA director William Casey wondered why Soviet agents were being called back to the Soviet Union and arrested.

It was not Ames's sloppiness as an agent that led the CIA to suspect him, however. Rather, it was his betrayals that first set the agency on his trail. Beginning in the summer of 1985, Soviet agents and double agents who worked for the CIA began running into trouble. Some were called back to the Soviet Union and arrested. Some simply vanished. Two of the first to go were Motorin and Martynov, whose names Ames had given away in April. The list grew throughout the fall. "What the hell is going on in Moscow?" CIA director William Casey demanded.[114] Other agents asked themselves the same question.

At first they attributed the betrayals to Edward Lee Howard, a disgruntled CIA agent who defected to the Soviet Union in 1985. Clayton Lonetree, a Marine guard who gave classified information to the KGB in Moscow in 1986, was also a possible cause of the trouble. The actions of those two did not explain all the losses, however. Howard and Lonetree had had no opportunity to betray some of the agents who disappeared. The agency eventually had to conclude that it had an internal problem. "I always knew that we could have a traitor in our midst," says CIA investigator Jeanne Vertefeuille. "I was not an ostrich with my head in the sand. Nor, I believe, were the people I was working with."[115]

Mole Hunt

The search for the identity of the mole proved long and complicated. About two hundred agents, Ames included, had to be investigated. A joint CIA-FBI task force created in 1991 first narrowed the field to twenty. Again Ames was included. His luxurious lifestyle and excessive spending—signs that he might be taking payoffs—were noted, although most people believed that his money came from Rosario's family in Colombia. "I encouraged everyone to think that Rosario was rich and I was living off her," he explained.[116] Like other suspects, he was asked to take lie detector tests. He managed to pass even though his responses were questionable at times.

Finally in 1992 investigators made a breakthrough. They discovered that Ames had a habit of having lunch with a Russian diplomat and shortly thereafter making a large deposit into his checking account. The linked events were highly significant. "It doesn't take a rocket scientist to tell what is going on here," a CIA investigator confirmed when she saw the evidence. "Rick is a . . . Russian spy!"[117]

The FBI began a lengthy surveillance of Ames. Covertly, they followed his car, wiretapped and searched his home, and sorted through his trash. It was frustrating work. Four times Ames made dead drops, made pickups, or contacted his handler without the surveillance team getting it on film. They worried that Ames or Rosario might discover they were being watched and that Ames might flee the country before they caught him.

Eventually, the FBI found evidence to prove Ames's guilt—a torn-up note in his trash that confirmed a rendezvous with the Soviets in Bogotá, Colombia. They also got incriminating conversations between Ames and Rosario, notes and telephone numbers, and messages in Ames's computer that he had thought he had deleted.

Capture

The FBI arrested Rick Ames on February 21, 1994, the day before he was scheduled to fly to Moscow for a top-level conference. Rosario was arrested as well since it was clear that she had known about and encouraged her husband's double-dealing. "I'm not saying that right off the bat she knew where the money suddenly started coming from," an FBI investigator says. "But she wasn't stupid. She had to know at some point something was wrong. She just chose not to know. The important thing was that the money was there. That's all she cared about."[118]

In exchange for leniency for his wife, Ames pleaded guilty to espionage and was sentenced to life in prison without parole. Rosario was given a five-year sentence. Even in light of her husband's sacrifice, she was not appreciative. "Not too many people are real men. They don't have the guts, the courage, the honor to be called a man, and I thought he was. He was not man enough to stop this from happening to me, to protect me."[119]

Retrospect

Despite the fact that Ames was the first spy to be caught without help of a Soviet informer, the CIA came under harsh criticism for its slowness in catching him. Many Americans were appalled that, during the time he was under investigation, Ames continued to have access to top secret information, continued to pass information to the Russians, and was responsible for the deaths of four more U.S. agents in the Soviet Union. The Ames affair, along with other agency problems, led to the early resignation of CIA director R. James Woolsey in 1994.

Other spies committed treacherous acts over the centuries, but Aldrich Ames will be long remembered for his greed, his lack of remorse, and the cold-blooded way he sent so many men to their deaths. Oleg Gordievsky, a KGB officer who was betrayed by Ames but escaped execution, says, "Rick Ames would have known exactly what he was doing in betraying the information: he was sentencing the victim to death. . . . He has the blood of a dozen officers on his hands. He would have had my blood, too, had I not managed to escape."[120]

EPILOGUE

Spies of Tomorrow

After the collapse of the Soviet Union in 1991, many people assumed that the need for spies was over. The KGB had been disbanded. The Cold War had drawn to a close. World leaders seemed to be coming together in a mood of greater openness and mutual support. Cooperation was the order of the day.

Less powerful nations and people, however, continue to pose threats to the world. CIA director R. James Woolsey stated in early 1993, "The threat of the dragon has been replaced by a jungle of poisonous snakes."[121] The danger from rogue dictators and malevolent terrorists has to be monitored before it can be controlled.

Industrial competition—the desire to have the latest technologies, the best marketing strategies, and so forth—creates the potential for spying among businesses and corporations around the globe as well. Jeffrey Richelson points out, "Thus far the United States has resisted the temptation to engage in purposeful industrial espionage for the benefit of American companies, but monitoring and neutralizing such activities by other nations has become a high priority of the CIA."[122] Obviously the need and desire to learn one another's secrets did not go away just because the Cold War came to an end.

Electronic Eyes

With the world so competitive, unpredictable, and even dangerous, espionage continues indefinitely. Experts point out that spies of the future may sit behind desks in intelligence headquarters, watching what goes on in other countries on the screens of their computers. Donald McCormick says, "This is the kind of espionage that is collected all the time by spy planes with electronic eyes, by satellites recording every detail their cameras can pick up and by a host of other electronic gadgets passing on information to a central computer system."[123]

Such spying can be safer and more efficient than human espionage efforts. It can take in more territory, cover longer time spans, and eliminate human risk and human mistakes. A good example of the strengths of electronic espionage involves events in the Middle

East in the 1990s. Before the Persian Gulf War of 1991, satellite photographs revealed thousands of Iraqi troops amassing along the Kuwaiti border, movement that would not have been easily noted by human members of the intelligence community. After the war, satellites detected equipment in Iraq for manufacturing nuclear weapons—equipment hidden from U.S. inspectors that might have been missed without America's spy technology.

The Human Advantage

Despite the strengths of high-tech espionage, there are still advantages to human spies. No satellite or spy plane can replace a Sidney Reilly or an Aldrich Ames when it comes to getting inside information hidden deep within a corporation or agency. No "spy in the sky" can measure up to agents like Elizabeth Van Lew and Kim Philby when it comes to evaluating the moods, motivations,

The use of computers, satellites, and other electronic devices will greatly contribute to spying techniques of the future.

and morale of a society. Says one CIA operative, "If you can get into the mind of the [men who threaten the peace] of the world, then you've got a weapon that no technical amount of information can give you."[124]

Technology has enhanced espionage, but there will always be spies as long as there are secrets to steal. The men and women who belong to the second oldest profession will not be out of a job anytime in the foreseeable future.

NOTES

Introduction: The Second Oldest Profession

1. Richard Deacon, *Spy!* London: British Broadcasting Corp., 1980, p. 7.
2. Donald McCormick, *The Master Book of Spies*. London: Hodder Causton, 1973, p. 85.
3. McCormick, *The Master Book of Spies*, p. 85.
4. Nigel West, *A Thread of Deceit: Espionage Myths of World War II*. New York: Random House, 1985, p. 1.
5. McCormick, *The Master Book of Spies*, p. 85.

Chapter 1: Mrs. Barnes

6. John Bakeless, *Turncoats, Traitors & Heroes: Espionage in the American Revolution*. New York: Da Capo Press, 1998, p. 252.
7. Quoted in Bakeless, *Turncoats, Traitors & Heroes*, p. 254.
8. Quoted in Bakeless, *Turncoats, Traitors & Heroes*, p. 256.
9. Quoted in Bakeless, *Turncoats, Traitors & Heroes*, p. 256.
10. Quoted in Bakeless, *Turncoats, Traitors & Heroes*, p. 257.
11. Quoted in Bakeless, *Turncoats, Traitors & Heroes*, p. 257.
12. Quoted in Bakeless, *Turncoats, Traitors & Heroes*, p. 258.
13. Quoted in Bakeless, *Turncoats, Traitors & Heroes*, p. 258.
14. Quoted in Bakeless, *Turncoats, Traitors & Heroes*, p. 260.
15. Quoted in Bakeless, *Turncoats, Traitors & Heroes*, p. 260.
16. Quoted in Bakeless, *Turncoats, Traitors & Heroes*, p. 361.
17. Quoted in Bakeless, *Turncoats, Traitors & Heroes*, p. 361.

Chapter 2: Crazy Bet

18. Quoted in David D. Ryan, ed., *A Yankee Spy in Richmond: The Civil War Diary of "Crazy Bet" Van Lew*. Mechanicsville, PA: Stackpole Books, 1996, p. 26.
19. Quoted in Ryan, *A Yankee Spy in Richmond*, p. 27.
20. Quoted in Ryan, *A Yankee Spy in Richmond*, p. 33.

21. Quoted in William Gilmore Beymer, "Miss Van Lew," *Harpers Monthly*, June 1911, p. 88. www.mdgorman.com/Miss% 20Van%20Lew.htm

22. Quoted in Ryan, *A Yankee Spy in Richmond*, p. 118.

23. Quoted in Harnett T. Kane, *Spies for the Blue and Gray*. Garden City, NY: Hanover House, 1954, p. 241.

24. Quoted in Ryan, *A Yankee Spy in Richmond*, p. 12.

25. Quoted in Jay Robert Nash, *Spies: A Narrative Encyclopedia of Dirty Deeds & Double Dealing from Biblical Times to Today*. New York: M. Evans and Co., 1997, p. 490.

26. Quoted in Kane, *Spies for the Blue and Gray*, p. 241.

27. Quoted in Kane, *Spies for the Blue and Gray*, p. 243.

28. Quoted in Kane, *Spies for the Blue and Gray*, p. 242.

29. Quoted in Ryan, *A Yankee Spy in Richmond*, p. 97.

30. Quoted in Ryan, *A Yankee Spy in Richmond*, p. 17.

31. Quoted in Kane, *Spies for the Blue and Gray*, pp. 248–49.

32. Quoted in Beymer, "Miss Van Lew," p. 86.

33. Quoted in Ryan, *A Yankee Spy in Richmond*, p. 20.

34. Quoted in Ryan, *A Yankee Spy in Richmond*, p. 122.

35. Quoted in Ryan, *A Yankee Spy in Richmond*, p. 22.

Chapter 3: Agent Extraordinaire

36. Robin Bruce Lockhart, *Reilly: Ace of Spies*. New York: Penguin Books, 1967, p. 7.

37. Quoted in Michael Kettle, *Sidney Reilly: The True Story of the World's Greatest Spy*. New York: St. Martin's Press, 1983, p. 18.

38. Lockhart, *Reilly: Ace of Spies*, p. 40.

39. Lockhart, *Reilly: Ace of Spies*, p. 65.

40. Quoted in Lockhart, *Reilly: Ace of Spies*, p. 71.

41. Lockhart, *Reilly: Ace of Spies*, p. 72.

42. Lockhart, *Reilly: Ace of Spies*, p. 83.

43. Quoted in Kettle, *Sidney Reilly*, p. 50.

44. Quoted in Kettle, *Sidney Reilly*, p. 137.

45. Quoted in Kettle, *Sidney Reilly*, p. 137.

46. Kettle, *Sidney Reilly*, p. 139.

47. Quoted in Norman Polmar and Thomas B. Allen, *Spy Book: The Encyclopedia of Espionage*. New York: Random House, 1997, p. 466.

Chapter 4: The Great Betrayer

48. Quoted in Phillip Knightley, *The Master Spy: The Story of Kim Philby*. New York: Alfred A. Knopf, 1989, p. 262.

49. Quoted in Knightley, *The Master Spy*, p. 29.

50. Quoted in Knightley, *The Master Spy*, p. 34.

51. Quoted in Knightley, *The Master Spy*, p. 36.

52. Quoted in Anthony Cave Brown, *Treason in the Blood*. New York: Houghton Mifflin, 1994, p. 334.

53. Quoted in Knightley, *The Master Spy*, p. 150.

54. Quoted in Brown, *Treason in the Blood*, p. 365.

55. Quoted in Knightley, *The Master Spy*, p. 128.

56. Quoted in Andrew Boyle, *The Fourth Man*. New York: Dial Press, 1979, pp. 390–91.

57. Quoted in Brown, *Treason in the Blood*, p. 432.

58. Quoted in Knightley, *The Master Spy*, p. 181.

59. Quoted in Knightley, *The Master Spy*, p. 217.

60. Knightley, *The Master Spy*, pp. 225–26.

61. Quoted in Knightley, *The Master Spy*, p. 269.

62. Quoted in Knightley, *The Master Spy*, p. 236.

63. Quoted in Knightley, *The Master Spy*, p. 257.

64. Quoted in Knightley, *The Master Spy*, p. 261.

Chapter 5: Undercover at Pearl Harbor

65. Takeo Yoshikawa and Norman Stanford, "Top Secret Assignment," *United States Naval Institute Proceedings*, December 1960, p. 30.

66. Yoshikawa, "Top Secret Assignment," p. 33.

67. Yoshikawa, "Top Secret Assignment," p. 33.

68. Quoted in Edward Oxford, "Intrigue in the Islands," *American History Illustrated*, July–August 1991, pp. 54–55.

69. Yoshikawa, "Top Secret Assignment," pp. 34–35.

70. Yoshikawa, "Top Secret Assignment," p. 35.

71. Quoted in Oxford, "Intrigue in the Islands," pp. 62–63.

72. Quoted in Gordon W. Prange, *At Dawn We Slept: The Untold Story of Pearl Harbor*. New York: McGraw-Hill, 1981, p. 472.

73. Quoted in Oxford, "Intrigue in the Islands," pp. 63–64.

74. Quoted in *Time*, "Remember Pearl Harbor," December 12, 1960, p. 23.

75. Quoted in *Time*, "Remember Pearl Harbor," p. 23.

Chapter 6: Atomic Bomb Spies

76. Quoted in Ilene Philipson, *Ethel Rosenberg: Beyond the Myths*. New York: Franklin Watts, 1988, p. 35.

77. Quoted in Philipson, *Ethel Rosenberg*, p. 80.

78. Quoted in Philipson, *Ethel Rosenberg*, p. 93.

79. Quoted in Michael Dobbs, "Julius Rosenberg Spied, Russian Says; Agent's Handler Contradicts Moscow in Controversial '50s Case," *Washington Post*, March 16, 1997, p. A1.

80. Quoted in Philipson, *Ethel Rosenberg*, p. 131.

81. Quoted in Dobbs, "Julius Rosenberg Spied, Russian Says," p. A1.

82. Quoted in Ronald Radosh, "The Venona Files," *New Republic*, August 7, 1995, p. 26.

83. Quoted in Ronald Radosh and Joyce Milton, *The Rosenberg File: A Search for the Truth*. New York: Holt, Rinehart and Winston, 1983, p. 67.

84. Quoted in Philipson, *Ethel Rosenberg*, p. 198.

85. Quoted in Radosh, *The Rosenberg File*, p. 71.

86. Quoted in Radosh, *The Rosenberg File*, p. 44.

87. Quoted in Radosh, *The Rosenberg File*, p. 47.

88. Quoted in Philipson, *Ethel Rosenberg*, p. 227.

89. Quoted in Radosh, *The Rosenberg File*, pp. 197–98.

90. Quoted in Radosh, *The Rosenberg File*, p. 189.

91. Quoted in Radosh, *The Rosenberg File*, p. 272.

92. Quoted in Radosh, *The Rosenberg File*, p. 280.

93. Quoted in Philipson, *Ethel Rosenberg*, p. 306.

94. Quoted in Robert and Michael Meeropol, *We Are Your Sons: The Legacy of Ethel and Julius Rosenberg*. Boston: Houghton Mifflin, 1975, p. 235.

95. Quoted in Jonathan Root, *The Betrayers*. New York: Coward-McCann, 1963, p. 283.

96. Quoted in Radosh, "The Venona Files," p. 27.

97. Quoted in Radosh, "The Venona Files," p. 25.

98. Radosh, *The Rosenberg File*, p. 453.

Chapter 7: CIA Mole

99. Quoted in Pete Earley, *Confessions of a Spy: The Real Story of Aldrich Ames*. New York: G. P. Putnam's Sons, 1997, p. 252.

100. Quoted in Earley, *Confessions of a Spy*, p. 34.

101. Quoted in Earley, *Confessions of a Spy*, p. 45.

102. Interview with Aldrich Ames, "Spies: Episode 21," CNN *Cold War* series, 1998, p. 2. www.hfni.gsehd.gwu.edu/~nsarchiv/coldwar/interviews/episode-21/aldrich1.html

103. Quoted in Earley, *Confessions of a Spy*, p. 94.

104. Quoted in Earley, *Confessions of a Spy*, p. 112.

105. Quoted in Earley, *Confessions of a Spy*, p. 110.

106. Quoted in Earley, *Confessions of a Spy*, p. 107.

107. Quoted in Earley, *Confessions of a Spy*, p. 130.

108. Quoted in Earley, *Confessions of a Spy*, pp. 145–46.

109. Quoted in Earley, *Confessions of a Spy*, p. 139.

110. Quoted in Earley, *Confessions of a Spy*, p. 177.

111. Interview with Sandy Grimes, "Spies: Episode 21," CNN *Cold War* series, 1998, p. 1. www.hfni.gsehd.gwu.edu/~nsarchiv/coldwar/interviews/episode-21/grimes2.html

112. Quoted in Earley, *Confessions of a Spy*, p. 286.

113. Quoted in Peter Maas, *Killer Spy: The Inside Story of the FBI's Pursuit and Capture of Aldrich Ames, America's Deadliest Spy*. New York: Time Warner, 1995, p. 132.

114. Quoted in Earley, *Confessions of a Spy*, p. 200.

115. Quoted in Earley, *Confessions of a Spy*, p. 224.

116. Quoted in Earley, *Confessions of a Spy*, p. 243.

117. Quoted in Earley, *Confessions of a Spy*, p. 301.

118. Quoted in Maas, *Killer Spy*, pp. 45–46.

119. Quoted in Earley, *Confessions of a Spy*, p. 286.

120. Quoted in Earley, *Confessions of a Spy*, p. 30.

Epilogue: Spies of Tomorrow

121. Quoted in Jeffrey T. Richelson, *A Century of Spies: Intelligence in the Twentieth Century*. New York: Oxford University Press, 1995, p. 428.

122. Richelson, *A Century of Spies*, p. 428.

123. McCormick, *The Master Book of Spies*, p. 175.

124. Quoted in "Spies," *Cold War*, CNN, March 14, 1999.

FOR FURTHER READING

Teri Martini, *The Secret Is Out: True Spy Stories*. Boston: Little, Brown, 1990. A collection of spies is discussed including John André, Belle Boyd, Mata Hari, and Kim Philby.

Tara Baukus Mello, *The Central Intelligence Agency*. Philadelphia: Chelsea House, 2000. A behind-the-scenes look at the CIA today.

Francis Moss, *The Rosenberg Espionage Case*. San Diego, CA: Lucent Books, 2000. Well-balanced, well-written account of the trial of Julius and Ethel Rosenberg.

George Sullivan, *In the Line of Fire: Eight Women War Spies*. New York: Scholastic, 1996. A history of women and espionage.

Burke Wilkinson, *Cry Spy! True Stories of Twentieth-Century Spies and Spy Catchers*. Englewood Cliffs, NJ: Bradbury Press, 1969. Stories of little-known secret agents who spied between 1900 and the Cold War.

Karen Zeinert, *Elizabeth Van Lew: Southern Belle, Union Spy*. Parsippany, NJ: Dillon Press, 1995. Biography of Richmond native Elizabeth Van Lew, who spied for the North during the Civil War.

John Ziff, *Espionage and Treason*. Philadelphia: Chelsea House, 2000. Includes the stories of some world-famous spies including Benedict Arnold, Kim Philby, and Aldrich Ames.

WORKS CONSULTED

Books

John Bakeless, *Turncoats, Traitors & Heroes: Espionage in the American Revolution*. New York: Da Capo Press, 1998. An account of espionage during the Revolutionary War, including descriptions of both British and American spies and important spy rings.

Andrew Boyle, *The Fourth Man*. New York: Dial Press, 1979. The story of Kim Philby, Guy Burgess, and Donald Maclean and how they became spies for the Soviets.

Anthony Cave Brown, *Treason in the Blood*. New York: Houghton Mifflin, 1994. Dual biography of Kim and Harry St. John Philby, whose unorthodox lives placed them at odds with the established British society into which they were born.

Richard Deacon, *Spy!* London: British Broadcasting Corp., 1980. Six true stories of espionage in the twentieth century.

Pete Earley, *Confessions of a Spy: The Real Story of Aldrich Ames*. New York: G. P. Putnam's Sons, 1997. An account of Aldrich Ames's life and career. The author interviewed Ames himself as well as numerous friends, family members, coworkers, and agents. Excellent primary quotations.

Harnett T. Kane, *Spies for the Blue and Gray*. Garden City, NY: Hanover House, 1954. Covers civilian spies of the Civil War, including a chapter on Elizabeth Van Lew, "Grant's Spy in Richmond."

Michael Kettle, *Sidney Reilly: The True Story of the World's Greatest Spy*. New York: St. Martin's Press, 1983. Brief, well-documented account of Sidney Reilly's life and career. Factual, but a little difficult to read at times.

Phillip Knightley, *The Master Spy: The Story of Kim Philby*. New York: Alfred A. Knopf, 1989. Biography of Kim Philby written just before his death. Knightley is the only Western journalist ever to interview Philby in depth. A clear, well-written account of the master spy.

Robin Bruce Lockhart, *Reilly: Ace of Spies*. New York: Penguin Books, 1967. Colorful biography of Sidney Reilly, written by the son of Sir Robert Bruce Lockhart, one of Reilly's fellow spies.

Peter Maas, *Killer Spy: The Inside Story of the FBI's Pursuit and Capture of Aldrich Ames, America's Deadliest Spy*. New York: Time Warner, 1995. The story of the discovery and arrest of CIA mole Aldrich Ames from the FBI's point of view.

Donald McCormick, *The Master Book of Spies*. London: Hodder Causton, 1973. The inside story of spying including the history of spying, how to become a spy, what spying is like, and spy tradecraft.

Robert and Michael Meeropol, *We Are Your Sons: The Legacy of Ethel and Julius Rosenberg*. Boston: Houghton Mifflin, 1975. Authored by the Rosenbergs' sons. Contains many personal letters written by their parents.

Jay Robert Nash, *Spies: A Narrative Encyclopedia of Dirty Deeds & Double Dealing from Biblical Times to Today*. New York: M. Evans and Co., 1997. Biographies of all major agents who have spied throughout time and around the world. Also includes information about major spy agencies such as the CIA and the KGB.

Ilene Philipson, *Ethel Rosenberg: Beyond the Myths*. New York: Franklin Watts, 1988. Focuses on Ethel Rosenberg as daughter, wife, and mother.

Norman Polmar and Thomas B. Allen, *Spy Book: The Encyclopedia of Espionage*. New York: Random House, 1997. An overview of spying, including world-famous and little-known secret agents, information on major spy rings, and explanations of common intelligence terms. Excellent.

Gordon W. Prange, *At Dawn We Slept: The Untold Story of Pearl Harbor*. New York: McGraw-Hill, 1981. Lengthy account of events leading up to the bombing of Pearl Harbor. Describes the role secret agent Takeo Yoshikawa played in the bombing.

Ronald Radosh and Joyce Milton, *The Rosenberg File: A Search for the Truth*. New York: Holt, Rinehart and Winston, 1983. Based on previously unavailable material, the book presents the Rosenberg case in a fair, well-balanced light.

Jeffrey T. Richelson, *A Century of Spies: Intelligence in the Twentieth Century*. New York: Oxford University Press, 1995. Includes chapters on the history of espionage organizations, spies during World Wars I and II, moles, technological espionage, and other topics.

Jonathan Root, *The Betrayers*. New York: Coward-McCann, 1963. An account of the Rosenberg case in which the author examines whether the two were great spies or merely Communist extremists.

David D. Ryan, ed., *A Yankee Spy in Richmond: The Civil War Diary of "Crazy Bet" Van Lew*. Mechanicsville, PA: Stackpole Books, 1996. The secret diary of Elizabeth Van Lew who spied for the Union during the Civil War. Includes a short biography of the spy.

Nigel West, *A Thread of Deceit: Espionage Myths of World War II*. New York: Random House, 1985. Examines a number of myths and misconceptions that surround spies and espionage operations of World War II.

Documentary

"Spies," *Cold War*. CNN, March 14, 1999. The *Cold War* series tells of the conflict between the United States and the Soviet Union between 1945 and 1991. The episode on spies includes archival footage and excellent first-person interviews with spies and spymasters.

Periodicals

Michael Dobbs, "Julius Rosenberg Spied, Russian Says; Agent's Handler Contradicts Moscow in Controversial '50s Case," *Washington Post*, March 16, 1997, p. A1. First person-account of Julius Rosenberg's espionage activities as related by his Soviet handler Alexander Feklisov.

Edward Oxford, "Intrigue in the Islands," *American History Illustrated*, July–August 1991, pp. 50–66. Overview of U.S. military strength in Hawaii in 1941 and of Takeo Yoshikawa's spy activities as he contributed to Japan's attack on Pearl Harbor.

Ronald Radosh, "The Venona Files," *New Republic*, August 7, 1995, pp. 25–27. The article discusses the Venona files, formerly classified documents that show Julius Rosenberg was a high-ranking spy for the Soviet Union.

Time, "Remember Pearl Harbor," December 12, 1960, p. 23. Short account of Takeo Yoshikawa's espionage activities in Hawaii in 1941.

Takeo Yoshikawa and Norman Stanford, "Top Secret Assignment," *United States Naval Institute Proceedings*, December 1960, pp. 27–39. Nineteen years after the fact, the Pearl Harbor spy tells the story of his top secret assignment to spy for the Japanese in Hawaii.

Internet Sources

Aldrich Ames, "Spies: Episode 21," CNN *Cold War* series, 1998. www.hfni.gsehd.gwu.edu/~nsarchiv/coldwar/interviews/episode-21/aldrich1.html. Transcript of interview with CIA mole Aldrich Ames, made during the taping of CNN's *Cold War* series.

William Gilmore Beymer, "Miss Van Lew," *Harpers Monthly*, June 1911. www.mdgorman.com/Miss%20Van%20Lew.htm. Early article relating the espionage exploits of Elizabeth Van Lew.

Sandy Grimes, "Spies: Episode 21," CNN *Cold War* series, 1998. www.hfni.gsehd.gwu.edu/~nsarchiv/coldwar/interviews/episode-21/grimes2.html. Transcript of interview with CIA investigator Sandy Grimes, made during the taping of CNN's *Cold War* series.

INDEX

PICTURE CREDITS

ABOUT THE AUTHOR

Diane Yancy works as a freelance writer in the Pacific Northwest, where she has lived for more than twenty years. She writes nonfiction for middle-grade and high school readers and enjoys traveling and collecting old books. Some of her other works include *The Hunt for Hidden Killers*, *Camels for Uncle Sam*, *Civil War Generals of the Union*, *Life in a Japanese American Internment Camp*, and *Life on the Pony Express*.